Building Virtual Reality with Unity and SteamVR

Building Virtual Reality with Unity and SteamVR

Second Edition

Jeff W. Murray

CRC Press
Taylor & Francis Group
Boca Raton London New York

CRC Press is an imprint of the
Taylor & Francis Group, an **informa** business

CRC Press
Taylor & Francis Group
6000 Broken Sound Parkway NW, Suite 300
Boca Raton, FL 33487-2742

© 2020 by Taylor & Francis Group, LLC
CRC Press is an imprint of Taylor & Francis Group, an Informa business

No claim to original U.S. Government works

Printed on acid-free paper

International Standard Book Number-13: 978-0-367-27265-4 (Hardback)
International Standard Book Number-13: 978-0-367-27130-5 (Paperback)

Visit the Taylor & Francis Web site at
http://www.taylorandfrancis.com

and the CRC Press Web site at
http://www.crcpress.com

To my boys: Never give up. Forget about the material and remember that if you do your best, you will always be a success to me. Also, be nice to the cat.

_____

Contents

Acknowledgments

H AVING PEOPLE AROUND ME who believe in my abilities and work makes a massive difference. To every person who has ever supported me, either personally or professionally, I want to say a sincere thank you. You are amazing.

I would like to extend special thanks to the people who believed in my work and helped me with their support: Michael Zucconi—senior public relations manager at HTC and thank you to the entire HTC Vive team. I love my HTC Vive with a passion, and I will always be an HTC Vive fan!

There are a lot of people who helped and supported my work and this book along the way—I'd like to extend thanks to everyone who helped including Brian Robbins, VR Martin, Chris Hanney, Technicat (for endless support and good vibes), Molegato, Mickael Laszlo, Juanita Leatham, CoolPowers, Dave Brake, Sigurdur Gunnarsson, Kevin Godoy R., Wim Wouters, IdeaFella, Liam Twose, RafaEnd, Lynxie, Alistair Murphy, Christer McFunkypants Kaitilla, Dani Moss, Vinh (the Actual Final Boss), Quantum Sheep, Scott Wilson, Huck Z (Overclocked), Paradise Decay, Kryten, Silverware Games, Pete Patterson, Mike White, Dr Oculus VR, Say Mistage, Andy Hatch, Sean MacPhedran, GermanRifter VR, Tony Walsh, Andreas "BOLL" Aronsson, Richard Bang, Cat, Darrel Plant, Cassie, Christopher Brown, Phil Nolan, Pixel Hat Studio, Vehicle Physics, Marcus Valles, Trev, Karyl, Hello Games (No Man's Sky in VR is a trip), Tami Quiring, Nadeem Rasool, Dwayne Dibley, Liz and Pete Smyth, Isaac and Aiden, Ethan and Will, David Helgason, James Gamble, Vasanth Mohan (FusedVR), Lister, Alexander Kondratskiy, Dan Hurd and Evan Reidland, The Oliver Twins, Jeevan Aurol, Rick King, Rami Ismail, Big Man, Aldis Sipolins, Ric Lumb, Craig Taylor, Rob Hewson, Dani Moss, Jayenkai (JNK), Pablo Rojo and Ryan Evans. I would also like to sincerely thank the codeMantra team and the whole team at CRC Press/AK Peters, including Jessica Vega and Rick Adams, for making this book a reality.

And to you, dear reader! Thank you for buying this book. I wish I could convey how awesome it is to know that someone else is reading this. The potential for VR continues to go beyond anything we have seen before; transcending format, convention, gender, and politics. The virtual world is open to new ideas and new ways of thinking and you, the creators, hold the key to writing the rule books and finding the magic in our new universes. It is already developing new perspectives and journeys for all of us, and I truly cannot wait to see what you create. I sincerely hope this book helps you to start your own virtual reality journey. Get in there, create new universes, and feel free to let me know when I can visit them!

Jeff W. Murray

Author

Jeff W. Murray is the author of *C# Game Programming Cookbook for Unity3D* (2014) and *Game Development for iOS with Unity3D* (2012) also published by CRC Press. An original Oculus Rift backer, Jeff is a true VR fan. He has extensive experience including working with IBM Research on cutting-edge VR research projects. He also self-publishes VR games on Steam and Viveport. In his game development career spanning over 20 years, Jeff has worked with some of the world's largest companies (including Sony, BBDO, and Microsoft) as a Game Director, Developer, and Game Designer. He has worked with the Unity engine since its initial public release, on projects ranging from hit mobile games to medical simulations. Jeff has a passion for playing sim racing games and devouring Jaffa Cakes.

Author

Prerequisites

To get started in VR with this book, you will of course need a VR-ready PC and whatever cool hardware tech you want to plug into it. Along with your chosen VR devices, let us take a quick look at what else you will be needing:

Example Unity Projects for this book: Download the example files that accompany this book from https://github.com/psychicparrot/BuildingVRWithUnityAndSteamVR.

Unity (available from the Unity store at http://www.unity3d.com): Unity and the required Software Development Kits (SDKs) can be downloaded free of charge with no catches. Unity Personal boasts that it is a fully featured version of Unity with just a few caveats. You can do everything in this book with Unity Personal. If you are unsure as to whether or not you need a paid version of Unity, you can always try out the free Personal edition to get used to it and see how it all goes before you put any money into it.

Steam client: The Steam client is a free download that gives you access to Valve Software's library and a store full of games. Essentially, Steam is an application that allows you to download and buy things, but in the context of this book, Steam is the application that you use to download and run SteamVR with.

SteamVR: SteamVR is a system based on Open Source Virtual Reality libraries. It provides a platform for VR. SteamVR runs as a part of the Steam client. Unity will communicate with your VR hardware through the SteamVR system.

C# programming knowledge: This is not a book about learning how to program for beginners. There are several other books out there for that specific purpose. Programming is a vast subject, and it makes no sense to try to show both programming and SteamVR development at the same time. I will be explaining how the code works, but you will need to know some C#.

Basic Unity knowledge: I aim for this book to be used with little Unity knowledge, and I hope that you can look through and utilize the example content no matter what level you are at. That said, I will not be teaching Unity techniques in this book, and if you are new and want to advance to make complicated VR experiences, you need to either follow the amazing Unity-provided tutorials online or pick up a Unity starter book.

WHO IS THIS BOOK FOR?

There is a basic Unity crash course in this book, but I do not go into detail. I will do everything I can to outline processes, keyboard shortcuts, and where to click to make the right things happen, but this is not a book to teach Unity or programming.

This is not a book about the right or wrong ways to write code. We assume that the reader has some experience of the C# programming language but may be completely new to VR or VR-focused development. It is important to note that I am a self-taught programmer and I understand that there may be better ways to do things. Use the concepts, make them your own, and do things the way you want to do them. Most of all, try to have fun doing it.

Introduction

IN 2017, WE STOOD at the gates of a new technological landscape. As we looked out at the virtual real estate trying to figure out just how and what to build there, it was obvious there is a lot to discover. In the virtual world there are no politics or borders to what we can experience and what we can build for others to experience. Just as early filmmakers had to find out how to tell their stories up on the cinema screen, we are only just beginning to explore the grammar of virtual reality (VR). Even the very basics of interfaces: how our fellow cybernauts interact with the virtual world, is still undecided. What is the grammar of VR? What feels natural in the virtual world? How do we move around, touch things, feel objects, and manipulate the environment? The number of people with access to the tools to create virtual content has never been so wide ranging, and we have more people than ever coming up with new and exciting additions to our virtual experiences. In the race to provide technology to accommodate new experiences, hardware manufacturers are running as fast as they can to make VR better, stronger, and faster. No matter how quickly we run to keep up, the technology does not stop evolving and changing. Technology will keep moving. We will never stop learning.

When you reach the end of this book, it will be up to you to get involved and to potentially start shaping VR's future. Do not be afraid to throw out convention and do things that are different to the ways we have interacted with games or simulations in the past. You are a visionary who could help shape the VR landscape of tomorrow. The virtual experiences of the future will be built upon the experiences of today, so experiment and create amazing new things! Remember to have fun, look after yourself, and be nice to each other.

CHAPTER 1

A Brief Introduction to the Virtual World

Virtual reality (VR) lets us interact with computer-generated worlds in completely new ways. The rules are only just beginning to be written. This chapter looks at VR from a bird's-eye view; we will look at how we got to the consumer VR technology we have today, what the challenges are, what is possible, and a little about what it means to be a VR developer in the current generation.

Some of the sections in this chapter would probably make for good books of their own, but this chapter is intended to provide grounding before we dive into the virtual world later on in this book.

HOW LONG HAVE WE BEEN VIRTUAL?

The term has been with us for a lot longer than you might expect. One of the earliest uses, most likely the first, was by the writer Antonin Artaud in his collection of essays "The Theatre and Its Double" published in 1938 (Artaud, 1958). Artaud referred to "The Virtual Reality of Theatre," which looks at the theater and the relationships between the actors and reality. Although Artaud was not talking about VR as we know it, I do feel that there are some interesting parallels between VR and the theater in terms of the presence and dramatic use of space. Artaud believed that the theater was a place where people would go to find a sense of humanity, a connection to the emotional beyond, and other media. In a way, he attempted to describe how theater created a sense of presence for the theatergoer through an emotional and psychological connection to the stage and its performers. In the virtual world, we would like visitors to feel a connection or a presence in perhaps a similar way to what Artaud described. In VR terms, an emotional and psychological connection is what we refer to as immersion or telepresence.

We must understand the environment around us, to find context for how the virtual universe works, and how we are supposed to interact with it. The lighting, the way things move, colors, and the world scale—the entire stage has a massive impact on how virtual visitors feel and the depth of experience they could have. Just as a stage play might guide the audience through a story with both visual and nonvisual cues, the virtual visitor will look to find a pathway, and it is up to the creators of virtual worlds to define that pathway, hone it, and discover interesting ways to help define our virtual experiences.

BEFORE THE HEADSET

The idea of simulating reality for training and entertainment has been kicked around for a long time. Long before actual VR, devices were invented that took on a similar function. In the early 1930s, for example, one of the first VR-like inventions was a device known as the Link Trainer. It was essentially a flight simulator using motors and mechanical devices to simulate the types of conditions a pilot might experience in the air. The Link Trainer helped train pilots to know how to compensate for varying weather conditions and to fly safely without having to risk a real aircraft.

VR was also something in the minds of science fiction writers and futurists. Some of them got it right, while others not so much. In the 1935 short story "Pygmalion's Spectacles," the science fiction writer Stanley G. Weinbaum imagined a pair of goggles that would provide holographic recordings for the wearer (Weinbaum, 1949). It would be a long time before anything even close to that prediction would make it to fruition, but thanks to "Pygmalion's Spectacles," the idea of being able to travel to other worlds through a headset or viewer had truly been born.

THE BIRTH OF THE HEAD-MOUNTED DISPLAY

Around four years after Stanley G. Weinbaum penned "Pygmalion's Spectacles," something called the View-Master Stereoscope appeared. It was a device for viewing photographs based on the principle of showing a different image to each eye to form a stereoscopic 3D picture. One interesting point about the View-Master is its similarities to today's Google

Cardboard, taking people to locations that they may not be able to visit in the real world—virtual tourism. That was not the only use for View-Master, however, as the U.S. military saw the potential in the 1940s, ordering around 100,000 viewers (Sell, Sell and Van Pelt, 2000).

The View-Master is still going strong, albeit in a few different forms. Mattel makes the regular View-Master binocular-type viewers and now a View-Master VR smartphone-based headset intended for educational and educational leisure use.

Though not directly related to the head-mounted display (HMD), Morton Heilig's Sensorama is widely regarded as the next milestone in VR after the View-Master. It was essentially a 3D cinema unit about the same size as an arcade cabinet. Patented in 1962, Sensorama featured stereo speakers, a stereoscopic 3D screen, a vibrating seat, and fans with smell generators so that viewers could even smell the action. Its inventor Morton Heilig was a filmmaker. He made all of the short films for Sensorama, and he tried to make movies that would give the viewer a feeling of being inside them. In one movie, the viewer would have the viewpoint as if they were on a bicycle ride through New York. The Sensorama would blow air into their face and make smells that were akin to the city. The 3D speakers roared out the sounds of the streets as the vibrating chair shook to simulate the feeling of the bumps in the road as they are hit by the wheels. Sensorama took its viewers and attempted to make them feel present inside the actual experience, rather than merely watching it on a screen. Sadly, Heilig's invention failed to sell, and with no investment, it never got any further than the prototype stages. Regardless of whether it was a success, the goal was very similar to what we would like our virtual worlds to do today.

This is the point where we come back to the HMD system. After Sensorama, Morton Heilig went on to work on something known as the Telesphere Mask—the first HMD. Its television screen was capable of stereoscopic 3D and was intended to be used for watching movies rather than anything interactive, which meant that motion tracking was not a consideration. Telesphere Mask was used only for noninteractive films, but it remains to be the first example of a HMD, representing a major step toward VR.

A year later, two engineers took the HMD concept and introduced motion tracking. Their system is called Headsight.

Headsight was the brainchild of Philco Corporation. It featured a magnetic tracking system and would show images on its cathode-ray tube (CRT) screen, live-fed from a closed-circuit television camera. The camera would move around based on the tracked position of the headset, which made the invention an interesting prospect for the military as it could be used as a remote viewer in situations where sending in a human might be too dangerous.

For the next major jump in tech, we skip forward to 1968 when Ivan Sutherland and his student Bob Sproull created The Sword of Damocles. You can find the phrase "Sword of Damocles" in all kinds of literature, ranging from Shakespeare to videogames and movies. The name refers to an ancient Greek anecdote, where Damocles trades place with a king only to discover that being a king is a much more dangerous and difficult job than he anticipated. The phrase is also used to express the ever-present danger those in power have to live with, such as a queen who fears someone else might like to forcibly take the throne from her, or perhaps the leader of a criminal gang who fears takeover from another criminal.

The Sword of Damocles was the first system to take a HMD and connect it to a computer to create the images. Though technology would only allow for basic wireframe graphics, I am sure that in 1968 entering this virtual world must have been a pretty mind-blowing experience.

VR systems were too expensive outside of military or research fields. In the mid-1980s, public interest in VR began to grow and hardware makers did begin to develop cheaper technology, but still not cheap enough for the home market.

VR arcade machines appeared in the late 1980s. Costing in excess of $50,000 each, they offered a basic experience with a headset and handheld controllers inside a vector-based simulation. The costs associated with the hardware kept VR out of reach for the general public, and it would not be until the 1990s when capable technology started to become affordable.

As a side note; it was not actually until 1987 that the term "VR" was used in the way we understand it today, despite Artaud having used the term nearly 50 years prior. Jaron Lanier, whose company Virtual Programming Languages (VPL) Research developed VR equipment, is credited as popularizing "VR" as an all-encompassing term for the field he was working in.

THE ROAD TO CONSUMER VR

One name you might be surprised to read about in the VR space is Sega. In 1993, Sega was riding high from its Sega Genesis game console when it announced something called SegaVR. SegaVR was intended to be an add-on for the Genesis. Launch titles included Virtua Racing and Matrix Runner, though it never came to be. After technical difficulties and reports of headaches and nausea during playtesting, SegaVR never launched. It was canceled in 1994 before consumers even had a chance to try it for themselves. The year 1995 was a milestone for this new affordable consumer VR market, though, seeing the arrival of the Nintendo Virtual Boy and the Forte VFX1.

VR had been riding high in the public eye throughout the 1990s. The VR scene had been trendy for a while and made appearances in major Hollywood movies that helped define a generation with its futuristic imagery. Many often regard the Nintendo Virtual Boy as having a key place in its advancement. Nintendo's VR outing was affordable, futuristic, and had some great launch titles, but it was a disaster. The media savagely attacked it, reporting that most players were experiencing headaches and nausea. It had many flaws including a low-quality, monochromatic display and an uncomfortable position you needed to be in to play on it. The technology was not good enough, and interest alone in VR was already starting to wane. Even in true VR experiences of the time, the types of display technology used back then were CRT displays with low refresh rates. The displays could not update fast enough to keep up with users' head movement. Early VR lenses were difficult to adjust, and HMDs from the 1990s were uncomfortable and bulky—some weighing as much as five pounds or more. Adding the pull from the heavy cables, you can quickly understand how little time it would take for a viewer's neck to get tired and painful. Low processor speeds, lenses that caused eye strain and headaches, laggy head tracking, and the widespread nausea and sickness were no doubt the biggest contributors to the steady decline of VR in the latter half of the decade. It made too many people feel sick. The technology was just not ready.

HOME PC VR

All the way back in 1995, there was a VR system intended for the home market that cost under $700. It was called the VFX1. Made by Forte Technologies, the VFX1 cost around $695, and its HMD was an impressive bit of kit that could play PC games like Quake, DOOM, Decent, and Magic Carpet in VR on a regular PC computer system.

The VFX1 was feature-rich; it had built-in headphones, a microphone, and head movement tracking on three axes (the same as the Oculus DK1). Its display may have been far from where we are today, but at the time it was spectacular with 256 color graphics rendering out to dual 0.7″ 263 × 230 LCD displays at 60 Hz. Before you go comparing those numbers to something like the current generation rendering at, say, 120 Hz 2,160 × 1,200 on organic light-emitting diode (OLED) screens, remember that games at that time were only rendering at lower resolutions anyway. Any higher resolution display, at that time, would have been an expensive waste.

Despite incredible technical specs and quality, the VFX1 failed to sell enough units to be viable. The exact reason for this is unclear, but it could have been down to the lack of computers outside of offices. Back in 1995, there were dramatically less computers in homes. Or perhaps it was PC specs? The very latest systems were running processors at around 133 MHz, but 3D acceleration cards were not commonplace (a VFX1 requirement). By late 1995, 3DFX had only just introduced the first home PC 3D graphics acceleration card, the Voodoo (3Dfx Interactive, 1995). Home PCs were also relatively expensive. A new PC with a Pentium Pro processor could cost upwards of $1000, and you still needed to pay another $700 on top of that for the VR headset. Sadly, neither the VFX1 nor its predecessor VFX2 was popular enough to keep their makers in the business.

CONSUMER VR REBIRTH

By the year 2000, the buzz around VR had fizzled out almost entirely. The technology had not been advanced enough to give the public what they expected from all the hype. There were still a few VR arcade machines available, but most hardware manufacturers had written it off as bad business. It would take another wave of technological advancement, in another field entirely, that would allow VR to make a return.

Oculus VR is an American technology company, founded in Irvine, California, by Brendan Iribe, Palmer Luckey, Michael Antonov, Jack McCauley, and Nate Mitchell in 2012. The first prototype of their VR headset, the Oculus Rift, was a real hack. It was made from a mobile phone screen wired up to some aftermarket components and taped together. All the technology to make this happen, and access to that technology, had come about at the right time. Advances in the market for mobile device technology had already pushed the development of essential components for headsets. All it took were some clever engineers to put the pieces together in the right way. Miniaturization of components for mobile devices, affordability, improvements in screen technology, gyrometers, and tracking hardware were big contributors to the birth of this new generation of VR devices.

The Rift was announced later that year as a Kickstarter crowd-funding campaign to manufacture VR headsets and supply to backers who pledged

$300 or more. The campaign was a massive success, raising $2.4 million—ten times their original funding goal amount. Over the next few years, Oculus shipped out two preproduction models to their backers: Oculus VR Development Kit 1 (DK1) and Oculus VR Development Kit 2 (DK2).

In March 2014, the social media giant Facebook acquired Oculus VR for $2.3 billion. A year later, HTC announced the HTC Vive VR system.

The first consumer-focused Oculus headset launched in March 2016—named the Consumer Version 1 (CV1). Like Oculus, it took HTC until 2016 to reach a consumer-ready version—3 months after the Rift's launch. The HTC Vive offered a similar spec headset as the Rift; however, the Vive also offered motion-tracked controllers (the Vive "wands") as part of the standard package. At that time, Oculus had no tracked controller solution and was shipped with an Xbox One wireless controller instead, but the company eventually answered back with their Oculus Touch controllers, launching late in 2016.

Today, there are many different headsets in the market, some taking different approaches to the technology. Starting at the low-end experience, you can buy something called "cardboard" VR for less than $20—this is a simple cardboard box framework containing lenses. To use it, a cell phone is slotted into the cardboard structure so that the lenses show the phone's display. Apps and experiences run on the cellphone, and interactivity comes in the form of a single button atop the box. Cardboard is ideally suited to short, simple VR experiences and videos, and is used primarily in education as a cheap way to engage students.

At the top end of the scale at the time of writing is the Varjo VR1—weighing in upwards of $9,000 for the headset. The VR1 boasts Bionic Display™ technology offering "human-eye resolution" and integrated eye tracking. VR1 is not aimed at home users and is intended for (quoting their website) "complex and design-driven industries like training and simulation, architecture, engineering and construction, and industrial design." However, as SteamVR supports the VR1 out of the box, there is no real reason why it should not be used for gaming.

Somewhere in the middle of the VR market is the Valve Index. It is a high- to mid-range VR solution that utilizes the Lighthouse tracking technology for room-scale experiences. One of the most outstanding features of the Index is its controllers (formerly known as Valve Knuckles controllers) which strap to your hands and have capacitive touch sensors to track pinky, ring and middle fingers. Index controllers also have pressure sensors that detect how hard you are squeezing.

The technology is moving fast, changing and evolving constantly as we try to solve some of its problems and make better VR experiences. In the three years since the first edition of this book was written, we have already seen some incredible changes in the landscape and the birth of a new type of VR headset: The all-in-one, which uses inside-out tracking to deliver VR experiences without having to have a PC or cellphone attached to them.

COMPLICATIONS AND CHALLENGES OF VR

For a long time, Hollywood painted an unrealistic view of the virtual world that may have raised expectations to impossible heights. Moviemakers represented VR as a technology that can take over the senses and make experiences indistinguishable from reality. To moviegoers, VR means photorealistic images, sounds, and methods of moving around with perfect reproductions of their real-world counterparts. To reach that, there are old and new problems to solve.

There are seemingly endless ways we can interact with the virtual world or ways that the virtual world can interact with the viewer and they all need figuring out. How do we interact with VR? Is the best solution to use our hands and bodies, or to use controllers combined with locomotion systems? What about our eyes? How can we tell what a viewer is looking at inside a virtual world? How can viewers "feel" objects in VR?

Right now, movement is an issue directly related to space. The best and most realistic movement VR has to offer is in room-scale, where one can move around the environment in a natural way. This means we need an empty space set up in our houses and that can be an issue for a lot of people. Until we can reach simulated movement, such as suspending users on wires somehow or perfecting treadmill tech, larger arena-scale experiences will be limited to arcades or laser-tag-like spaces designed specifically for VR.

A VR headset can swap out your vision, but all the other senses—smell, taste, touch—we struggle with.

Latency

The term "latency," in reference to VR technology, usually refers to something called motion to photon latency. In layman's terms, this is the delay between the speeds at which the screen updates versus the speed that the person viewing the screen moves their head at.

The mind has no problem at all making sense of things at over 100 milliseconds of latency time, but it makes for an uncomfortable experience. The brain is not easily fooled into believing that an image is reality. It takes just the tiniest difference between how quickly you turn your head and what you see in the display for it to become a major contributor to an uncomfortable experience.

Many believe that an acceptable latency rate is below approximately 20 milliseconds. The lower we can get this number, however, the better. Current generation devices deliver between 10 and 20 milliseconds, but this number is only made possible with optimization techniques to do some clever estimations or "cheats" to update the display quicker.

Due to the delay between the computers running the simulation and the ones doing the calculations, even measuring latency is problematic at this level. To measure VR latency, developers have been known to use high-speed video to capture both the motion and the simulation, and the two videos are compared by stepping frame by frame through the video.

Juddering and Smearing

Computer graphics cards render with frames, normally at a rate so fast that our eyes do not see any sort of break or discrepancy between updates. The problem with VR is that we are building an interface that needs to work extremely closely in sync with the physical body. The display is trying to "trick" the brain into believing that it is seeing something unreal.

Whereas a monitor only renders a limited field of view, HMDs aim to surround the viewer with a wide field of view intended to replace real-life vision. It may not seem like it, but the speed at which you can turn your head and move your eye in the same direction can bring up perceptual problems caused by the eyes seeing in-between those frame updates. Having the wider field of view means that your eyes need to travel longer distances than they might with a traditional monitor, which is why it becomes more of an issue with HMD displays.

Frames are updated at a fixed rate, at fixed intervals in time, whereas the real world updates smoothly and consistently. When the eyes move faster than the display, there is no built-in system for our brains to fill in the gaps between frames.

The Screen Door Effect

The screen door effect gets its name because the effect is as if you are looking out through a screen door into the virtual world. In a headset, this is caused by a blurring of color around the pixels, the separated colors red, green, and blue, which are normally invisible but are made visible by the magnification the lens does to get the required view and focus on the headset's display.

Thankfully, once you get into VR and start engaging in some good VR content, the screen door effect becomes less of an issue. The effect may be there, and we may know it is, but the content usually takes your mind off it enough to just enjoy the experience.

Newer headsets such as the Valve Index, which uses a RGB subpixel array display, have found ways to cut down on the screen door effect by using a higher pixel density than Rift or HTC Vive headsets.

VR Sickness

VR sickness has plagued the VR industry from the start. Even the National Aeronautics and Space Administration (NASA) has not found a fix-all solution despite a lot of research. We may not be able to cure it, but there are certain helpers and methods you can apply to help lessen its grip on your virtual visitors.

VR Space

Tracking

"Room-scale" VR is the freedom to walk around a real-world space and has the hardware to track your position in it, and then represent your position in the VR simulation. In 2016, the HTC Vive was the first commercially available headset to offer room-scale tracking in up to a 15 × 15 foot radius.

The HTC Vive uses sensors built into the headset to detect laser beams. The base stations (also known as Lighthouse units) cast out a sweep of beams that cover the room. The Vive's many built-in sensors detect the beams and, based on which sensors are hit, angles and so forth, it calculates the headset position and rotation. The Oculus Rift CV1 uses the reverse of that—replacing the Lighthouses with cameras—where several infrared LEDs are lit on the headset and picked up by the camera view. The positions of the infrared LEDs, relative to the camera, are used to calculate the headset position and rotation. Both approaches have their advantages and disadvantages, and both approaches present huge challenges to overcome to be able to expand the play area space. Newer, all-in-one VR solutions, like the HTC Vive Cosmos, now offer an alternative method of tracking movement that may be able to solve large-scale tracking issues for good. Just a few years ago, at the time of writing the first edition of this book, a large-scale tracking system could cost in excess of $15,000. In 2019, a solution for large-scale tracking can cost just a few hundred dollars.

Location-Based Entertainment

Up until 2019, large-scale VR experiences utilized backpack computers as PCs to provide the hardware support and processing. Backpack computers are computers, similar in size and weight to laptops, made specifically to be carried as a backpack. Warehouse-sized experiences such as those offered by The Void (https://www.thevoid.com) allow people to move around a 1:1 scale fantasy world in VR. The Void offers what their website calls "… real-time hyper-reality that combines interactive sets [and] real-time effects." One of their experiences is called Star Wars: Secrets of the Empire, where players are disguised as storm troopers on a mission to retrieve important intel by solving puzzles and blasting their way through the VR universe.

Tracking Infinite Spaces

In the first edition of this book, the only solution to tracking in large-scale VR spaces was to use a complicated network of tracking sensors to watch where people are, and backpack computers, carried by the user and connected to each person's VR headset and controllers. In 2018, both Oculus and HTC have announced new stand-alone products that have tracking built right in—with no need for external sensors. This means a user can grab an HTC Focus Plus headset and wander as far as the headset tells them to—potentially infinitely sized worlds. This new wave of headsets uses something called inside-out tracking, whereby the headset has cameras mounted on the front, which are used to scan the surroundings and build up a virtual picture of the real world. How that virtual picture moves and changes provides the information to track player movement to relay back to the simulation. Essentially, the cameras on the front of the headset do the work we previously had to have sensors to do.

For larger scale experiences, developers are also combining marker-based tracking and inside-out tracking to increase reliability and accuracy. Using both methods cuts down on drift or tracking errors that may occur when using inside-out tracking alone.

Movement

If you do not have a large space available, but you still want to move around realistically in VR, there are a few other options. One answer may be motion platforms; players wear special shoes, and their feet slide around the platform as though they are walking. The motion platform detects the movement and uses that data to move them around in the virtual world. The biggest restriction of the motion platform is that players must be "held" in place, and the sensation is different to walking.

As well as motion platforms, treadmills are another proposed solution to the movement problem. Companies like Infiniwalk are developing treadmills, or moving floors, that allow players to walk or run around naturally. The treadmills move so that, despite leg movement, the players stay in place.

A final mention must go to CyberShoes, which takes a different approach to VR movement. Perhaps the lowest cost solution—certainly cheaper than treadmills or motion platforms—Cybershoes has players attach wheels to their shoes. Players sit on a swivel chair and use their legs to scoot around in a similar way to how I like to propel myself around my office on my wheeled chair when no one else is around! Small wheels on the shoe attachments are turned as the player rolls them against a carpeted area around the chair. That physical movement is translated into movement inside the VR simulation.

Input

Body Tracking

Cameras have been used for a long time in motion capture for 3D animation and videogames. Microsoft's Kinect cameras have achieved success in the home market by shipping with Xbox consoles as methods to interact with games and interfaces. With Kinect, players could act out bowling or tennis, and their movements would be duplicated by an avatar in-game. Camera-based motion capture techniques have been used to try to achieve full-body tracking suitable for VR with limited success. Single camera motion capture is difficult because of losing sight of certain parts of the body during specific poses or turns, and multiple camera motion capture soon gets expensive and complicated. Even professional motion capture normally requires "clean up" of the animation it captures, as it can be jittery and have incorrectly captured rotations.

Vive Trackers

HTC makes the Vive Tracker, which is a small hockey puck-shaped device that utilizes the Vive's Lighthouse tracking sensors to be tracked in VR. It has a small mounting point, the same standard-sized screw hole used by cameras and tripods, used to attach it to other objects such as tennis rackets, baseball bats, and so on—practically anything can be turned into a VR peripheral as long as the software can support it. By combining and wearing Vive Trackers, you can also track leg and body movements, too. One tracker on each foot and a third on the midsection of the body is enough to capture the data for full-body motion in VR, and some experiences already support this type of setup, including Island 359 via its VirtualSelf avatar system.

Motion Capture Suits

Motion capture suits offer another method of capture, and there are an increasing number of flavors available including, but not limited to:

Noitom's Perception Neuron V2 motion capture system uses gyroscopes, accelerometers, and magnetometers to track movement.

TeslaSuit offers haptic feedback, motion capture, temperature control, and biometrics all-in-one system. Embedded electroencephalography (EEG) and Galvanic Skin Response sensors capture vitals and stress levels.

Hand Tracking

Initially, Leap Motion was intended to be used as an alternative to the computer mouse. Rather than using the mouse to move the pointer around the screen, Leap Motion allows users to use hands and fingers to point at the screen and use gestures.

The HTC Vive team offer an application programming interface (API) to enable hand tracking with their Vive Pro and Vive Focus headsets (https://developer.vive.com/resources/knowledgebase/vive-hand-tracking-sdk/). At the time of writing, the quality of hand tracking achievable with this on the Vive Pro is not as good as the Leap Motion. The author did not have the opportunity to test this with a Vive Focus.

Eye Tracking

Companies such as HTC, Fove, Tobii Tech, and SMI believe that eye tracking has an important place in VR's future. With eye tracking, the computer detects where the viewer is looking and feeds that information back into the simulation for processing. In 2019, HTC launched the Vive Pro Eye, a version of their Vive Pro VR headset with eye tracking built in. The Vive Pro Eye is intended for enterprise users (business) and not aimed at the home market, but I wonder how long it will be before we see this technology find its way into consumer VR. Going on the incredible price drop of eye tracking technology over the last 3–4 years, I have a feeling that, if the demand for home VR continues, it will not be too far into the future.

This type of technology could be particularly helpful in social VR, where face-to-face meetings are important, or for advanced interactions with nonplayer characters. Eye tracking also has potentially game-changing implications for people with physical disabilities, by making it possible to control and interact just by looking.

Performance can also be improved by eye tracking. If we know where the eye is looking, the central focal point could be rendered at the highest resolution with anything outside of peripheral vision rendered at lower resolutions. This system of rendering only the focal point at a higher resolution is called foveated rendering.

Feeling VR

Tracking the physical body will help in making VR feel more real, but what about touching, feeling, or being physically affected? Many regular game controllers give you haptic feedback in the form of vibration from the controller. You might have felt this on Playstation or Xbox controllers. The vibration features can be used to give virtual objects the feeling of a physical presence. For example, I was recently playing a game where the player holds a sword and a shield. The sword was controlled by the right controller and the shield on the left. If I tried to put the sword through the shield, there was nothing that the game could do to stop me, but it did provide vibration whenever the two objects collided with each other. This small amount of feedback served to highlight what was happening, and it made the objects feel like they had some kind of physical presence rather than just being images of the objects I was looking at.

Other haptic feedback systems range from gloves that help you "feel" objects (normally by using different amounts of pressure restriction in finger movement) to body suits that make you feel impacts such as projectile hits.

DESIGNING AND DEVELOPING FOR VR

If you already have a game design document, or plans on how you intend to implement all of the interactivity in your virtual world, there is a very good chance that the final working systems will end up quite different from those original ideas. Testing and iteration are going to be at the very center of your production process and what feels right will triumph over anything that may have seemed right on paper.

With VR development, the best preparation you can do is pure prototyping: prototyping interactions, movement systems, and the scales of your environments—prototype everything until it feels right. Some companies even go so far as to build mechanics out of cardboard, in the real world, before even setting foot in VR. VR games company Schell Games calls this practice "brownboxing" (Greenwald 2018). Brownboxing is a great way to design and test VR interactions and interfaces without having to spend the time programming them and building 3D models.

Plan: Any Sort of Plan Is Better than No Plan!

Although VR development should be focused on prototyping and iteration, tasks can be outlined to a reasonable degree to help keep the project on track as well as to keep a sense of progression as you build out the experience.

My approach to project management starts at an overhead view. An outline of the project—just a single pager—is enough to get started. Once I have an outline that myself and everyone else involved in the project is happy with, I start to break that outline down into a bullet-point list of sections. From there, I can break down each section into their own bullet-point lists containing a list of items of what needs to be done to make that section happen. From there, if I need to, I can move down another level to make new lists of what needs to be done to accomplish each of those bullet points and so on until I have most of the project planned out. At the very least, I break the project down until I have enough of a plan to see what it's going to take to complete.

Once I can see all of the systems I need to build, I can see the approximate scope of the project and I can also think about areas that may cause problems before I hit them. Note that none of this is particularly detailed—just a list of jobs. I can break them down as much as I want, or leave them at a bird's-eye view of a particular area wherever I see fit—for example, areas that I know need a lot of prototyping will usually take the form of an overview at this stage, but may be broken down as the details become clearer.

When you have an idea of the systems required for your project, the main advantage is that you know right from the beginning where your strengths and weaknesses are. By breaking down the tasks which seem to be the most intimidating, each one can be split into manageable pieces or you can spend more time working out how to construct them.

The online service Trello (Figure 1.1) has been life changing for my projects and small project development practices. It is a free service, with a feature-rich premium paid offering if you find you need more functionality. Trello uses a card system to help you stay organized. Each card can be thought of as a task. Within that task, you can add a description or a checklist of subtasks. Earlier, I wrote about how I split my projects into bullet-point lists before moving forward. Now I take those bullet-point lists and turn them into Trello cards (Figure 1.2).

The way I like to organize my projects is to have columns for each stage of development. I always begin a project with the following named columns:

Issues: A list of current issues (also known as bugs). It is empty at the start of the project.

Now (or sometimes "In Progress"): I use this column for anything currently being worked on. Obviously, it is empty at the start of the project.

Next: This column contains all of the cards at the start of a project, then they are moved around. When I prepare the board, I put all of the cards here.

Completed: Cards that are completed. Empty at project start.

Always: Sometimes I call this column Repeating. Essentially, anything that repeats like a generic card for "Bug fixing" or "Refactoring code" goes here.

A typical day starts with a visit to the Trello board to grab a card from the "Next" column. I drag the card out of "Next" and place it in "In-Progress." Anyone else on my team can log into Trello and see my shared board. They can see what I'm working on at a glance of the "In-Progress" column.

Sometimes cards will be "In-Progress" for several days or jump back into the "Next" column and back again. That is fine. It is perfectly fine to move cards in and out of columns, especially when working in an iterative style. Sometimes, my cards come back out of the "Completed" column too—often multiple times as requirements change or extra functionality is required in some areas of the project.

Trello can also help teams see what needs to be done and what other members of the team are working on. A typical flow might be that a team

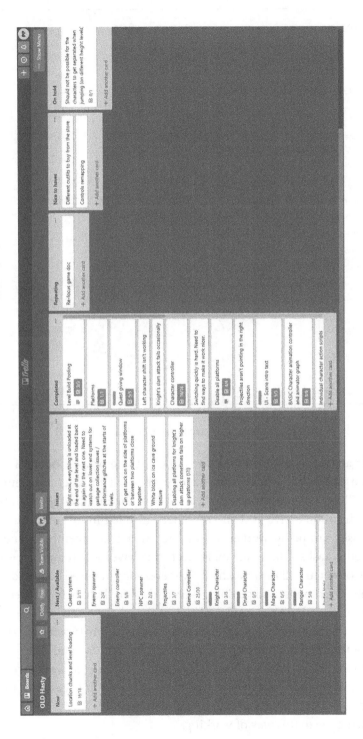

FIGURE 1.1 My typical Trello layout for a videogame project.

FIGURE 1.2   A card from one of my game projects, Axe Throw VR.

member arrives at the computer for work in the morning, opens Trello, and chooses a task to work on for that day. The card for that task is moved into the "Now" column to show they are working on it. Other members of the team soon arrive at their computers, also log in to Trello, and see which tasks are being worked on by the other team members, and so choose other tasks to take care of. Projects that have more than one person working on them will flow much better if everyone involved has an idea of what they are supposed to be doing—or, at the very least, which direction they are supposed to be running in!

On solo projects, Trello helps me to stay focused. My typical day starts with opening Trello, choosing a job to work on that day and dragging it over into the "Now" column. Every day, I find something to work on easily and quickly without having to search for tasks to do. It is easier to move forward each day. Thanks to my colleague from IBM, Aldis Sipolins, for introducing me to this way of working.

Get Your Main Interactions in Place Early

Early iteration of your core mechanics and testing on as many devices as you can get your hands on can save you time in the longer run. For example, if your project calls for the use of virtual power tools you should start the development process by figuring out how the tools will work, how a user switches between different tools, and how this applies to the environment and experience.

When I was developing my game Axe Throw VR (Figure 1.3), a VR game where players throw a variety of different sized and shaped axes at targets, it may seem obvious, but I started with the axe-throwing mechanics first. As the most important mechanic of all, I knew throwing had to be right. Getting the weight to be distributed so that axes would fly in a realistic manner took quite a lot of experimentation and prototyping. Once the axes could fly realistically, I then needed to pull back the realism to make the game more accessible to a range of skill levels and to make the game easily accessible to social environments like VR parties or a VR arcade.

I also discovered that Oculus Touch controllers deal with velocity differently to the Vive wands that I had been developing with, and so had to rebuild the core throwing code from the ground up to address it (quick tip: if you do write your own throwing code, you need to average out velocities over a number of frames rather than taking the velocity value from the controllers!).

FIGURE 1.3   Axe Throw VR by PsychicParrot is available on Steam and Viveport.

Once I had the axe-throwing mechanics set up for Axe Throw VR, I built a main menu system that would utilize the axes—a moving conveyor of targets for each menu item. Players throw an axe at a target to choose a menu item. Making the players throw axes at the menu means that the "how do I play" learning process happens in a very natural, easy to understand way without the use of a formal tutorial. Once the player has operated the menu, they have already begun to master the skills needed to play the game.

Test, prototype, and iterate on your core controls before going full steam ahead into production.

Test on Real People

Your team may be the best at what they do, but no one will be able to break your experience in the same way a novice user can. What tends to happen during testing is that you focus on particular areas and follow particular paths through the experience based on our own expectations of our users. New users will try things that you may not expect them to, which can often lead to finding issues that may even have been hidden in plain sight.

Another advantage to having other people test (other people not involved in production) is in seeing how their instincts align with yours. The way in which your interaction systems work will be pushed by users new to the experience and you will soon be made aware of problem areas by unpredictable usage.

If you know other VR developers, they may be able to bring another technical perspective to your project, but for a true picture, test with both experienced and inexperienced users.

Look for Combination and Flow

Switching modes, game states, or virtual equipment should be a part of a larger flow through the entire experience. The way everything works in the virtual world should have a level of cohesion to it, relying on a consistency of ideas across multiple systems. Users bring along their own conventions and expectations based on other experiences—and regardless of whether those experiences come from real-world activities or simulations or videogames, we can leverage them to make for a smoother transition to the virtual. Many of the conventions we see from game controllers, such as which buttons do what in racing games, have come about through a shared opinion that those are the best ways of doing things. Not just because of opinions, but that the way we can switch modes or change the game state flows so well when these conventions are applied.

Make sure that it is easy to switch from one item to another, if you expect users to do the same. Ensure that when you switch from one system to another that there is consistency. This consistency makes it easier for users to transition between them. For example, changing from a laser blaster to a light saber might have the same method to switch on or off the power.

Realism Is Not Always the Most Realistic

Just because something is realistic in terms of math or physics does not mean it will feel good in the virtual world.

In the early stages of development, the axes in my game Axe Throw VR felt more like axe-shaped balloons than anything made of metal or iron and the action of throwing axe had a sort of empty feeling to it. The axes did have the correct weight distribution and they moved through the air correctly, but there was something missing in the feeling of throwing them. They looked like axes and flew like axes but didn't feel like axes. We cannot (given the available technology) physically feel the weight of an object to lift or the sensation of that weight leaving our hands. In fact, for some of the larger axes in the game, I am not even sure that players would want to feel their real weight, but there needs to be some kind of connection with held objects.

In early experiments, one thing I tried was to attach axes being held to a spring, connected to the hand, rather than attaching axes directly. The spring allowed the axe to lag behind a little, with the intention of simulating weight. This had a degree of success in simulating weight—axes did feel more or less weighty depending on how much they lagged behind the controller. Sadly, this method also reduced the accuracy in the throwing mechanism and did not feel at all how you would hold or control a throwing axe in the real world.

Rather than trying to simulate weight, I wanted to see if it were possible to highlight the connection between the player and the axe instead. I asked: what does an axe need to do? It needs to be picked up, aimed, and thrown at targets. When players pick up or throw an axe, the sensation needs to be something physical as well as visual. When throwing the axes, how could I make it feel as though something was leaving the hand?

I chose two methods to "trick" players into feeling a connection to the axes. Those were:

1. A very short, medium intensity haptic buzz to the controller when an axe is grabbed/picked up. This acts partly as a physical confirmation of the action of "picking up" as well as helping to establish a physical relationship between the axe and the player's hand.

2. When a player releases an axe to throw it, there is an intense but short haptic buzz to the controller. This buzz is of a higher intensity than the buzz from picking up and several milliseconds longer, with the intention of placing more emphasis on the throw than on the action of picking up. I emphasize the throw more because, in my opinion as a game designer, that is where all the fun is and where the connection matters most.

Although very subtle and relatively simplistic, two haptic buzzes were all it took to dramatically improve the whole core interaction of the entire game. By highlighting the physical relationship (albeit an unrealistic one lacking physical weight) and creating that physical connection between the object and the hand, I found all Beta testers reported a huge improvement in the simulation of weight.

In summary, study the function of your virtual interactions. If you cannot simulate them accurately, or an accurate simulation does not help to further the goals of the environment/game/experience, try to find methods that highlight those actions yet suit the experience. Another example of this logic is the perceived power of a throwing mechanism. Often in VR, we find it useful to use an arbitrary multiplier for throw velocity—essentially making players stronger than they are in the real world—and it works because it fits into the context of the simulation, not because it matches real world physics.

Do not be restricted by reality. Do not feel as though realistic simulation is the only way to make your virtual world feel real. That "feeling" of reality will be contextual to the reality you create.

RECAP

In this chapter, we took a journey into the past to find out how VR made its way from military and scientific simulation to the consumer market in 2019. Before we all proclaim that VR has learned from its earlier mistakes and is now ready to take over the world, we looked at some of the main problems that are either unsolvable or still in the process of being solved. The full Holodeck experience is not quite there yet, but it is very much on the road to getting there.

We looked at some helpful methods for preparing and planning your VR projects and tips for how to go about development. Above all else, the best method for creating VR content is: Experiment and test. Then repeat. Then, repeat again, until everything feels right.

In the next chapter, in preparation for heading into Unity and VR in upcoming chapters, we look at safety, comfort, and suggestions for a healthy VR experience.

CHAPTER 2

Healthy VR Experience

I N THIS CHAPTER, THE AUTHOR ASSUMES THAT YOU have already set up your virtual reality (VR) hardware as per the manufacturer's setup instructions. Please follow the setup instructions carefully to ensure you have a safe VR play area.

Before we jump into the virtual world, this section of this book is intended to draw your attention to some important things to watch out for on your journey and to prepare you for healthy VR experiences in the future.

WHAT IS INTERPUPILLARY DISTANCE AND WHY SHOULD I CARE?

You may have seen the term Interpupillary Distance (IPD) used in VR. When hardware manufacturers use this term, it refers to the relationship between the distance between the lenses on the headset and the distance between the viewer's eyes. The Valve Index, HTC Vive, Vive Pro, and Rift include an IPD adjuster, and it is important that you set this correctly for the most comfortable experience. The short of it is that if the IPD is not set right, this may cause eyestrain and some discomfort.

There are two types of IPD you need to know about: real IPD and virtual IPD.

Real IPD

The real IPD is the distance between the viewer's eyes in the real world (Figure 2.1). This is the measurement you need to know for setting the IPD on your headset. On the Rift, alignment software features a visual section that guides you through the process of correct IPD alignment.

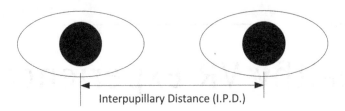

FIGURE 2.1 The real IPD.

On the HTC Vive and Valve Index, you will need to measure this yourself and adjust the headset (Figure 2.2) to a number. It is not too difficult to find out what your IPD is, and the benefits outweigh the inconvenience, so I highly recommend you take the time to do this properly. If you have more than one person using the HMD regularly, I would also suggest keeping a list of IPD settings for each person—perhaps just jot the numbers and names down in a notepad as I do, or save them into a text file on a computer or cellphone.

How to Measure Your IPD
By far, the easiest way to measure your IPD is with an app. If you have a newer smartphone, you should be able to find an app that uses the phone's camera, such as EyeMeasure on the iPhone X or newer, or Acer IPD Meter on Android, but you may need to print out a Quick Response (QR) Code to use the Android one. On a laptop or desktop machine with a webcam,

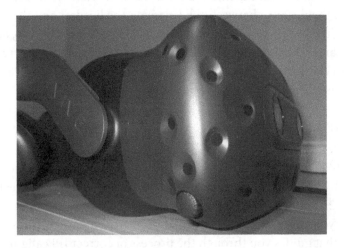

FIGURE 2.2 The HTC Vive and Vive Pro headsets have an IPD adjustment knob on the side.

you may also be able to find a browser-based IPD measuring app that takes a picture of you and uses a credit card or same-sized card to gauge scale. Be careful not to allow any app to take pictures showing the front of a debit or credit card or any important details such as your account number, signature, or security numbers. Just in case.

To measure your IPD without a smartphone, you can either visit an optometrist, who will measure it using a special device, or you can do it yourself with a mirror and a ruler or some sort of measuring tape. You may also find that you can do this with a home improvement tape measure or digital caliper, but for these instructions, we will stay low-tech.

To measure your own IPD manually:

1. Stand in front of the mirror. Hold the zero part of the measure below your left eye and extend it out past your right eye. Keep the measure straight, rather than following the contours of your face.

2. Close your right eye. Make sure that the zero end of the measure is directly below your pupil, in the middle of your eye. Keep still.

3. Close your left eye and look at the measure under your right eye. The mark directly underneath the center of your right pupil is your IPD.

Virtual IPD

The virtual IPD is the distance between the two cameras used to represent the viewer's eyes in the virtual world. With the SteamVR library, the virtual IPD is automatically taken care of. Its default settings will be matched to the real IPD. You may be wondering what this has to do with scale? Well, it turns out that we can change the perceived scale of the virtual world by adjusting the virtual IPD to something other than the real IPD. By changing the scale of the virtual eyes (the cameras used by Unity in the VR scene) we can make the viewer feel as though they are anything from looking up at large architecture on an epic scale all the way down to looking at a tiny toy village. With SteamVR, scaling the virtual IPD is as simple as scaling the main camera in the Scene. Note that it is not recommended to do as your simulation or game is running. Once it is set in the scene, it is best to just leave the camera scale alone during runtime. The visual effect of changing the IPD is very uncomfortable, particularly for viewers who may be sensitive to VR sickness.

Knowing When to Stop (the Telltale Signs of Oncoming VR Sickness)

Extensive studies by the military, the medical profession and even NASA have still not led to a cure for VR sickness. We do not yet know exactly how to tackle it, and VR sickness is a real thing that affects a great number of people in many different ways. Some of the most common types of sickness-inducing experiences are: first-person shooters, driving or flying simulators, cut scenes with a forced movement camera, or any sort of experiences where the camera twists or rotates a lot.

Remember that VR sickness is not something you can just "power through." Persistence will not make it go away. You will not be able to push through sickness and come out feeling good. It gets worse the longer you keep doing whatever is causing it, which means that the only way to stop it is to walk away and come back to VR once the ill feelings are gone.

Later in this book, we will look at some of the known techniques for reducing and avoiding sickness triggers. VR sickness affects different people in different ways, and it is triggered by different factors in different people, too, which makes providing a definitive list of symptoms almost impossible. What we can do is look out for some telltale signs that may be your body's way of telling you to take a break.

Important Note: This is not medical advice. If you need medical advice, please consult a medical professional. I'm a VR developer, Jim, not a doctor!

Dry Eyes

If you feel as though your eyes are drying out, that could be the beginning of eyestrain. First, take off the headset. If you have not already set up your IPD correctly, refer back to the "General Installation Hints and Tips" section and follow the steps to do so.

Eye drops may be a good way to make the experience more comfortable. I keep eye drops handy and use them every now and then before I put on the headset. A qualified optometrist/optician may be a good option if you find your eyes giving you trouble in VR.

If you have dry eyes, take a break.

Sweating

Sweating is not just central to your cooling system, it is also a way of the body trying to rid itself of poisons or sickness when the brain thinks that the body is under attack. Sweating is a very common symptom of VR sickness and the only way to stop it is to take a break. Preferably a break in a cooler space.

Try to keep the room to a comfortable temperature if you can, as wearing a headset can get hot quickly and exacerbate symptoms. Even more so if the VR experience is physical. Try to keep the temperature a little cooler than usual to allow for the extra heat generated by movement.

If you are sweating any more at all than usual, take a break.

Aching

What can I tell you about this? If you are experiencing any sort of pain, you need to rest. Rest well until it goes away completely. If the pain is intense, consult a healthcare professional. Eat well, fruits and veg. Look after yourself. VR can be surprisingly tiring. When you are new to it, build up your time in VR slowly.

If you are aching, you probably know what is coming here; take a break.

Nausea

Getting dizzy or feeling sick is never a good thing, but for many of us it is a regular part of the VR experience. If you start to feel sick at all, you should stop immediately and remove the headset. Take a break and see if it subsides before going back in. Sickness symptoms can last for more than a full day after you have been in VR. If you feel extreme nausea, the best way to combat it is to lie down and sleep. Always consult a medical professional if the problem gets worse or if you have any question as to its cause.

Take a break.

Headache

There are so many different reasons you could experience a headache that it may or may not be related to the VR experience. If you are getting headaches regularly from the headset, it may be eyestrain or related to your vision. Consult an optician or medical professional, as you may need corrective lenses.

Regardless of the cause, take a break if you get a headache.

Take Breaks

Take a 10-minute break every 30 minutes and a 30-minute break if you are playing for over an hour. At this stage, VR is still in its infancy. We should try to be cautious.

If in doubt, restrict your VR sessions to 10 minutes per day until you start to get a feel for your personal limits.

For children under 12, VR is not recommended by hardware manufacturers. Younger children's eyes are still developing, and who knows how a headset could affect that?

My kids like to try out VR and, from time to time, I do let them but I restrict VR sessions to a very short time (10–15 minutes) to be safe.

Eat, Drink, and Be Virtually Merry!

Keep a bottle of water nearby during all of your time developing or playing in VR—it does not have to be anything fancy, just as long as the water is clean. I got my water bottle from the drugstore and I fill it from the tap before I sit down. Drink plenty, regularly.

Eating right before going into VR is generally not a great idea if you suffer from VR sickness, as doing so may exacerbate nausea. If you find yourself prone to sickness and you get hungry, try to eat good, healthy food an hour or so before you use VR and avoid rich or sugary snacks that might make you feel sicker.

Do Not Break Your Back Making VR Things! Test Carefully

In the next chapter, you are going to be diving into Unity and creating a VR experience. As you progress, you will need to test numerous things along the way such as object interactions, space limitations, scale, and so forth. Before we go ahead with that, I want to talk a little about safety. As I write this, a good friend of mine has injured his back during VR testing and I would hate for you to do the same. Developing for VR, especially room-scale, can be a risk. I am not trying to scare, but it is well worth considering how you test, how you move around, and how you can be a little more cautious during testing. Check the space regularly to keep it clear of obstacles, watch out for cables trailing across places where they might pull things off desks (like cups, etc.) when you move around and prepare yourself for physical activity.

When you want to test something quick, it is easy to grab the headset or controller and make bad movements because you are half watching the screen and half the hardware. Not paying full attention to the hardware can mean hitting controllers against walls, dropping the headset or knocking things off the desk. Before you test with the hardware, stop and count to 5 as you consider the space around you.

Also, I know it takes a few seconds extra to put on the wrist straps, don the headset, and so on, but if your movements are going to be physical you should take the extra time. If not just to help protect your hardware investment.

Wherever possible, try to make your experience compatible with mouse and keyboard so that you can test small features without having to don the headset and anything else you might be using (controllers, VR gloves, haptic suits, etc.). The novelty of the experience will wear off relatively quickly once you have tested it over and over, day after day. When it does, it is too easy to shortcut to testing without consideration for your environment.

In room-scale VR, pay strict attention to the Chaperone/boundaries. A developer friend of mine recently destroyed a monitor with a Vive controller as he was so immersed in a game battle.

Be aware of the fact that you are holding expensive equipment that will sometimes negatively affect your sense of balance and space around you. A second of unforeseen dizziness caused by a technical issue, such as camera lag, can also be enough to knock you off-balance.

If you are making a room-scale experience that is particularly physical or taxing on the body, you may even want to do some warm-up or stretching before you start developing for the day. Room-scale experiences need your body to work, making the risk of a back injury or muscle injury a real prospect. This is serious stuff—you are dealing with body movement and you can sprain muscles, hit things, drop things, or even fall over. VR can be more physically demanding than you think. As you are testing your experiences, you will be exercising. Like all exercise, take care. Please do not break your back making VR things!

RECAP

In this chapter, we looked at setting up your VR environment and examined some tips for a healthier experience, such as calculating your IPD rating (very important for avoiding eyestrain and potential headaches!) and knowing when to take a break.

In the next chapter, we will take a crash course in the Unity editor by looking at its views and panels.

CHAPTER 3

Getting Set Up for Unity SteamVR Development

I N THIS CHAPTER, THE AUTHOR ASSUMES THAT YOU HAVE ALREADY SET up your virtual reality (VR) hardware as per the manufacturer's setup instructions.

INSTALLING STEAMVR

Once your hardware is set up, you need to download the required software. You will need both the Steam client software and the additional SteamVR download for all of the examples in this book. All the examples are targeted for SteamVR, and they use the SteamVR SDK for Unity. One of the biggest advantages of using SteamVR is the cross-platform compatibility between headsets, but there are many more advantages like the SteamVR Interaction system, which we will be looking at throughout this book.

In the next section, we will look at installing the Steam client, the SteamVR additional download, and then open Unity to see how easy it is to get the SteamVR SDK up and running in a basic project.

INSTALL THE STEAM CLIENT

To get SteamVR you first need the Steam client software. Traditionally used for purchasing and installing games, Steam has grown to feature all kinds of software and now VR libraries and apps. It is necessary to download the Steam client first, to be able to install SteamVR and all the games and software SteamVR requires.

Download Steam from your web browser: http://store.steampowered.com/.

Look for the Install Steam button somewhere along the top of the main page. The installation process is a standard Windows installer and should be straightforward. Follow the on-screen instructions to get Steam.

SET UP A STEAM ACCOUNT

Everything you need is free, but you do need a Steam account.

Start Steam and follow the instructions for setting up a new account or logging in with your existing account.

INSTALL STEAMVR

Once you have an account set up and the Steam client software running, you need to download and install SteamVR. Find this as a separate download within the Steam client, in the Library > Tools section. Right click on SteamVR and click Install Game.

START STEAMVR

Once SteamVR has downloaded and installed, open Steam and you should see a little VR icon in the top right of the window. Click the VR icon to start SteamVR. After a short time, the SteamVR status window should appear—see Figure 3.1. You will need to turn on your controllers, too, if you have not already.

The SteamVR status window (Figure 3.1) shows connected devices as well as their status. Everything shown in the SteamVR window should be green. Otherwise, if there are any problems with your headset, tracking or controllers, a colored icon or text-based message will let you know about the problem right away. The SteamVR status window will also inform you about any required firmware updates.

FIGURE 3.1 The SteamVR Window.

In Figure 3.1, you can see that I had my headset, two Index controllers, two lighthouses, and an Xbox controller connected. Unfortunately, my right controller was low on power, so a small icon (looks like a lightning strike in a circle) shows that it requires charging. You may see different icons depending on your own hardware setup, as the icons are loosely based on the appearance of their real-world counterparts.

SETTING UP A UNITY PROJECT FOR STEAMVR

Unity is free to download and one of the easiest game engines to use. The Unity editor (Figure 3.2) is where you create, configure, and bring to life all your graphics, sounds, music, and other elements that go to make up your virtual world.

In this book, we focused primarily on using SteamVR as the Software Development Kit (SDK). SteamVR is free, with the added advantage of being easy-to-use and supporting just about anything compatible with Open Source VR (OSVR) like the HTC Vive or Valve Index headsets.

To use SteamVR as a developer, as discussed earlier in this chapter, you need the Steam client software and SteamVR running. In Unity, you also need the SteamVR SDK imported into your projects. Before we get to that, for the benefit of readers who have not tried Unity before, there will be a quick crash course into the basic interface of the editor. If you know about Unity and you have already used it, feel free to skip ahead to the "Creating a New Unity Project" section to get started with our first project itself.

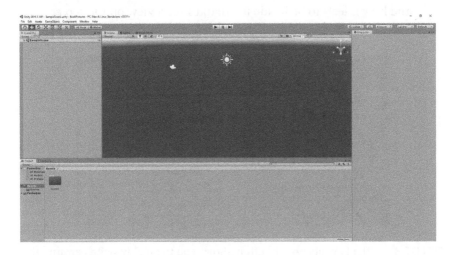

FIGURE 3.2   The Unity editor in its default layout.

DOWNLOADING UNITY TO MAKE A NEW PROJECT

If you have not already downloaded Unity, you can grab it from the Unity website at https://unity3d.com/get-unity/download.

UNITY EDITOR CRASH COURSE

This is not an extensive view of the Unity editor, and I am aiming for accessibility rather than in-depth analysis. If you require more information on the editor, Unity provides great documentation on their website (https://unity3d.com/learn/tutorials/topics/interface-essentials).

Editor Views and Panels

There are several different presets to help you find the best layout configuration for your own workflow. The presets are a great way to make Unity your own, but for this book I will be using the 2 by 3 layout instead of the default one that Unity starts with.

Choose the 2 by 3 layout preset from the dropdown menu in the top right of the editor window (Figure 3.3). The view will apply the change.

The Unity editor is split into different views and panels. In Figure 3.4, I have highlighted the following sections:

Game View: The Game view displays what Cameras in your Scene can "see," providing a preview of what the game world will look before it runs. In VR development, I find that I refer to the Game view less and less, as it is more important to see how everything looks in VR—and how it feels to be inside it—than to see a view on the screen.

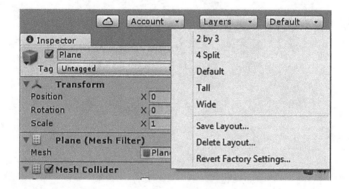

FIGURE 3.3 The Layouts preset button allows you to quickly switch around the layout of the editor.

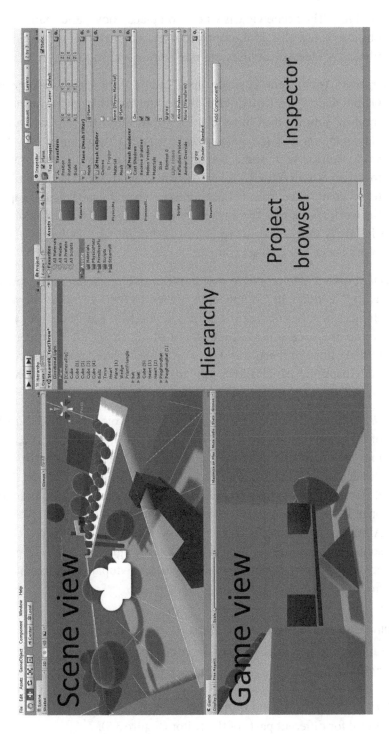

FIGURE 3.4   The Unity editor, broken up into sections.

Scene View: The Scene view is where you place, move, and manipulate objects visibly. This window provides a visual method for the manipulation of objects (rotation and positioning and so forth).

Hierarchy: Your Scene is made up of many different GameObjects. GameObjects are Unity's placeholder entities that go to form the meshes, sounds, and other elements that build the virtual world. GameObjects and the relationships between them affect how the world works, with some GameObjects linked to others, moving together or individually. The structure of your Scene is shown in a text format in the form of the Hierarchy—a text-based visual map of the world. Note that there is also a search function at the top of the Hierarchy that will come in handy for finding GameObjects whenever a Scene starts to get complex.

Inspector: GameObjects have position information, scale, and rotation as well as different Components applied to them to make them do things when the engine runs. Some Components are made from your scripts and code, other Components are built-in to Unity. Any configurable values, properties and so on, will be displayed in the Inspector. The Inspector panel allows you to inspect the currently selected GameObject's Components and alter any available properties.

Project Browser Window: Essentially, a Unity project is a huge bunch of files. You need to be able to do all sorts of things to the files, like move them around, edit them, and organize them, and so forth. The Project panel (I call it the Project browser) is where you can do that. It has a preview system so that you can see a file without having to open it—something that is essential for dealing with larger projects. All the images, sounds, and scripts you need for a major project can soon mount up and the Project browser is designed to help your project stay organized. Note the search bar at the top, too, which makes finding files easier.

Terminology and Common Use Things

There are a few general-use parts of the editor that fall outside of the views and panels.

Main Toolbar: The toolbar is made up of seven different tools, which are useful for different parts of the editor (Figure 3.5).

FIGURE 3.5 The toolbar.

From left to right, the toolbar is made up of

Transform Tools: Every GameObject has something attached to it called a Transform Component. The Transform gives us information about position, rotation, and scale of the GameObject. The Transform tools allow you to move, rotate, and manipulate the GameObjects visually in the Scene view; changing a GameObject's Transform in the Scene (Figure 3.6).

The hand icon (1) is used for moving the camera. The little crossed arrows icon (2) is for moving objects. The two arrows in a circle icon (3) are for rotation. The small box with four arrows coming out of it (4) is for scaling objects. Finally, the icon that looks like a circle with a cube around it (5) is the Rect Tool. The Rect Tool is a multipurpose tool primarily aimed for manipulating 2D graphics, such as user interface (UI) or 2D game sprites, but it can be handy sometimes for 3D objects too.

Transform Gizmo Toggles: On the left is the Pivot toggle. On the right, the Pivot Rotation toggle. The state of these toggle buttons affects how objects will react when you move or rotate them. The Pivot toggle decides the point that the object rotates around. The Pivot Rotation toggle switches from Local to Global world space (either tool handles work in global rotation or the active object's rotation).

Play/Pause/Step Buttons: Play/Pause/Step buttons control the simulation preview.

Cloud Button: The little cloud icon accesses Unity Services (things such as cloud-based storage and so on).

Account Menu: You need an account to use Unity (free or otherwise), and you can access account settings via this icon.

FIGURE 3.6 The transform tools.

Layers Menu: Layers are used by the Unity engine to decide how collisions affect each other. The Layers menu lets you create and edit layers.

Layout Menu: We already saw the Layout dropdown earlier, to switch from the Default Unity editor layout to a 2 by 3 layout.

Unity Terminology

Scenes: Unity splits its worlds into Scenes. Scenes work as you might imagine they would, acting as holders for all of the entities that make up a scene of a game. You can switch between Scenes at runtime to move between different environments, for example.

Components: Components are made either from your scripts, or built-in to Unity. They provide behavior to GameObjects such as collisions or sounds, and Components are added to GameObjects.

GameObjects: Think of GameObjects as empty entities that make up the entities in a game or simulation inside Unity. By assigning Components to GameObjects, such as Components to render objects or resolve collisions, GameObjects become the players, enemies, and worlds in a Scene.

Transform: The Transform is a Component that Unity automatically applies to all GameObjects. It contains information about position, rotation, and scale. We communicate with the Transform Component whenever we need to move, turn, or change sizes of objects.

Prefabs: You will often find that you need to create preconfigured GameObjects or groups of GameObjects at runtime, for example projectiles or particle effects. Prefabs are files that can contain one or more GameObjects with Components attached and Components configured, that you can add to your Scenes at any time.

Tags: Unity provides Tags to help you organize and identify GameObjects. In the Unity editor, you set up Tags with names (such as Player, Enemies, Terrain, and so on). In code you can use Tags to find or identify GameObjects.

Layers: The collision system is the main intended use for Layers. In the editor, Layers are given names, but in code we often refer to them by index number. Unity also allows you to choose the Layers that will be allowed to collide with each other via the Physics Manager's Layer

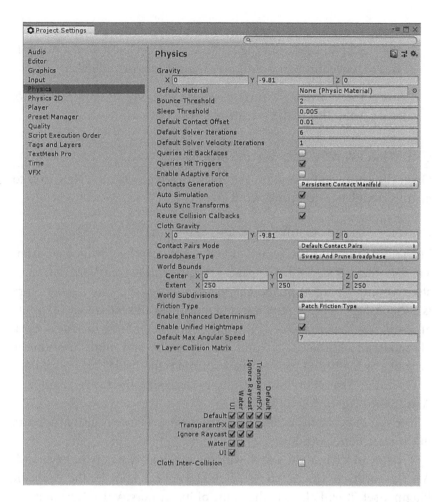

FIGURE 3.7 The Layer Collision Matrix allows you to choose which Layers can collide.

Collision Matrix (Figure 3.7), which is accessible through the menus Edit > Project Settings > Physics.

Triggers: Unity allows its collision system to register, but not actually attempt to resolve a collision, between two GameObjects. By checking the IsTrigger checkbox on a collision Component, such as a Box Collider, the game engine will register when the collision happens but not do anything physically to resolve it. You can add functions to your own scripts that will be called automatically by the game engine whenever these events occur, so that you know when a collision happens, and react to it in a custom way. As an example of usage,

Triggers are often used to tell when a player crosses a checkpoint—the checkpoint exists in the Scene as a GameObject, and a player is free to move through it without having its physics affected.

Canvas: The Canvas is a surface we use in Unity to render UI onto, when using Unity's UI system.

CREATING A NEW UNITY PROJECT

Open the Unity editor and on the splash screen, select the New icon to begin a completely new project.

Downloading the SteamVR SDK for Unity

The required files to use SteamVR with Unity can be downloaded from Valve's SteamVR Github page (https://github.com/ValveSoftware/steamvr_unity_plugin) or the Unity Asset Store. The Unity Asset Store is a shop where you can purchase and download all kinds of useful assets and scripts for your projects. Products on the Asset Store include scripts, 3D models, full projects, textures, and graphics, and more. The store is provided by Unity and you can get to it from right inside the Unity editor.

Open the Asset Store inside Unity by accessing the menu Window > Asset Store (Figure 3.8).

The search field runs across the top of the Asset Store page that appears in the main editor window.

Type SteamVR into the search window and press enter on the keyboard. After a short time, the search results should appear. Look for the SteamVR Plugin asset (it will also say the name of its creators, Valve Corporation, just underneath the image). If you have any trouble finding it, the SteamVR libraries are categorized under the Scripting section. Using the name of the category as an extra keyword may help to narrow down your search.

Click on either the SteamVR graphic (Figure 3.9) or the name "SteamVR Plugin."

In the top right of the product description you will find the Download button (Figure 3.10). Click on Download and then let Unity download it.

When the download has finished, the button will change to Import.

Click the Import button.

Unity will start importing SteamVR. Before the files are copied over into your project, a small window will appear prompting you to look at the files contained in the package (Figure 3.11). On an empty project, the extra step may seem pointless to check that it is OK to import the files. When you are

FIGURE 3.8 The Unity Asset Store opens in the main editor window.

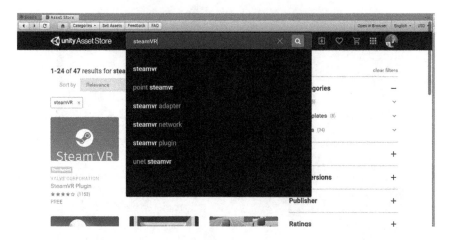

FIGURE 3.9   The Asset Store search results, showing the SteamVR Plugin.

FIGURE 3.10   The SteamVR Plugin asset store product description.

updating libraries to new versions in the future, or importing assets that you may have modified, this step becomes important as you might not want the asset package being imported to overwrite existing files in your project.

As we do not have anything else in this project just yet, you can go ahead and let Unity import everything.

Click the Import button.

Setting up SteamVR in Unity

The SteamVR team have done an excellent job in automating the setup for Unity. If the project settings are not quite right, a popup will appear to tell you all about it. The SteamVR settings window (Figure 3.12) tells you exactly which settings will be changed and what they need changing to.

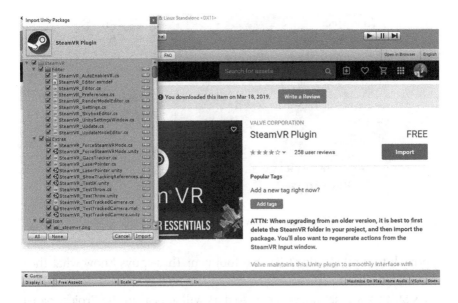

FIGURE 3.11   Unity checks with you that the files it will import are correct before it imports assets.

FIGURE 3.12   The SteamVR settings window helps you to make sure that your project is ready for VR.

Click the Accept All button.

SteamVR will automatically change the project settings. When the process is complete, a message appears saying something along the lines of "You've made the right choice!" The developers take a lighthearted

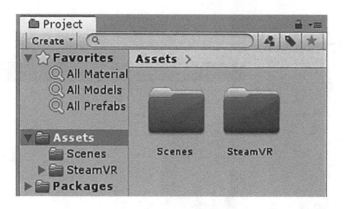

FIGURE 3.13   SteamVR adds two new folders to your project.

approach to it all but don't let that fool you: These guys know what they are doing!

As SteamVR is set up, two new folders will appear in the Project panel (Figure 3.13): Plugins and SteamVR. Any API suitable for working with the hardware go into the Plugins folder, and all the Unity code, examples and so forth, go into the SteamVR folder.

You can go ahead and close the Asset Store window. We are done with that for now.

In the Project browser, find the SteamVR > InteractionSystem > Samples folder. Inside Samples, double click on the Interactions_Example Scene.

The interactions example Scene is a little place where you can teleport around and try out some of the interactions that SteamVR has to offer (Figure 3.14). Put on your headset, power up the controllers and press the Play button in the center of the editor window to try it out.

Uh-ho … if you are running SteamVR 2.x, the first thing you'll see will be an error popup saying "It looks like you haven't generated actions for SteamVR Input yet. Would you like to open the SteamVR input window?"

Before we can continue, you need to set up the input system for SteamVR to know how you intend for users to interact with your experience.

Setting up SteamVR Input

SteamVR has an input system that is designed to work with any type of VR-compatible input device, so there is a little setup to do before we can get started. Click Yes.

Any other popup messages? Yep, this time it says "It looks like your project is missing an actions.json. Would you like to use the example files?"

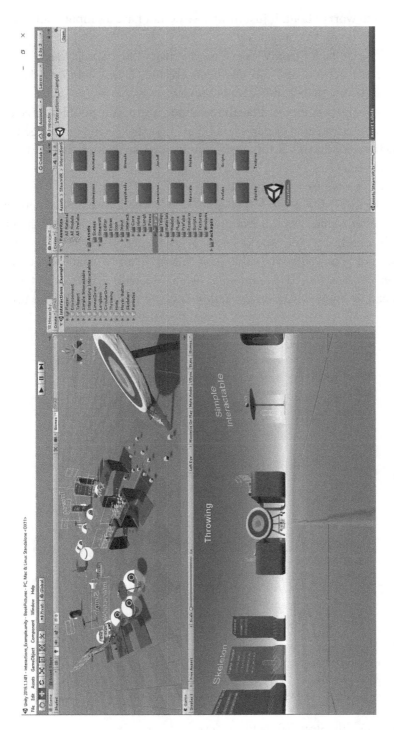

FIGURE 3.14 The SteamVR Interaction example scene.

Nothing to worry about. It just means we do not have an input configuration file set up for the project yet.

Click Yes to have SteamVR generate one from the example files.

Once the actions.json file has been created, a new window should appear in Unity, the SteamVR Input window.

If you happened to press Play in the editor, again, you would be greeted by yet another warning popup saying that "It looks like you haven't generated actions for SteamVR Input yet. Would you like to open the SteamVR Input window?"

Click Yes—we are not done yet!

The SteamVR Input window (Figure 3.15) is where we can map actions to controller inputs. Say, for example, that you wanted to have an action to grab something. You would set up a "grab" action in the input window and in your code. We will look at this in detail in Chapter 5: Using a Laser Pointer for UI Interactions, when we will write a script that will need to know whenever an action is being carried out by the user.

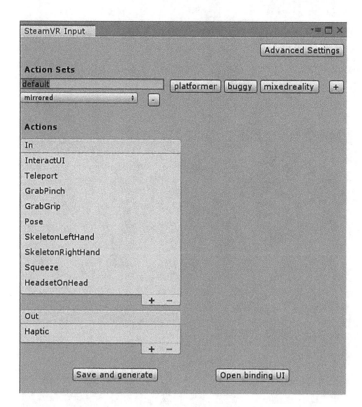

FIGURE 3.15   The SteamVR Input window.

When we breakdown the script for adding interactivity to a UI laser pointer, the bindings system will be key to making it work.

Click Save and Generate to finalize the input settings and generate the data SteamVR needs to run. It may take a short while to compile. Once compilation is done, you will be asked to save the scene.

Click Save and let Unity save your work so far.

After a little time, as Unity saves out the SteamVR config info, the SteamVR Input window will return. Close the SteamVR Input window, for now.

Have some fun and check out the Scene. Welcome to VR!

A ROOM WITH A VR VIEW

Now that you have wandered around some of the things that the Interaction system provides, it is time to set up your own Scene. In this section, we will add SteamVR to an existing Scene containing a 3D garden environment. There is nothing particularly complex—it is a garden environment and you can stand in it. This exercise should serve to demonstrate how straightforward it is to add VR functionality to a Unity Scene. To create the garden environment, I used the amazing free voxel-based 3D modeling software MagicaVoxel (https://ephtracy.github.io/), and I highly recommend it for building with voxels.

All the 3D models and project files for this book are included in the example files, which may be downloaded free of charge from the Github repository for this book at https://github.com/psychicparrot/BuildingVRWithUnityAndSteamVR.

Download and Extract Example Project Source Files

If you have not already extracted the example files into a folder on your hard drive, extract them somewhere where you can easily access them.

Open the example project for Chapter 3.

Adding SteamVR to an Existing Scene

With the example project for this chapter open, in the Project browser find the Assets folder and double click on the main_scene Scene to open it. We will add the VR camera next.

The SteamVR package includes some prefabs to help get things moving. One of them is a camera rig all set up and ready to go. FYI: The term "rig" is used by developers to describe a setup. In this case, that setup is made of GameObjects with Components attached to them and configured.

In the Project browser, find SteamVR > Prefabs. Inside that folder is a prefab named [CameraRig]. Grab [CameraRig] and drag it over to an empty space in the Hierarchy. Drop it there to add the new camera set up to the Scene. That is all we need to do to get SteamVR working in the Scene. Before continuing, however, we should take a quick look at what the [CameraRig] contains and why.

The SteamVR Camera Rig

Hold down the ALT key on the keyboard, then in the Hierarchy, left click on the little arrow to the left of [CameraRig]. This will expand out [CameraRig] to show its child objects. It looks something like this:

[CameraRig]

    Controller (left)

        Model

    Controller (right)

        Model

    Camera

Starting from the top, we have the [CameraRig] GameObject itself. If you click on it, you will see in the Inspector that it has a Component attached to it named SteamVR_Play Area. What this does is draw the blue frame around the play area.

The next GameObject down, a child under [CameraRig], is Controller (left). The Controller (left) and Controller (right) GameObjects are essentially the same. This will render the controller models in the virtual world to show where the real-world controllers are—Controller (left) and Controller (right). There is a single Component attached to these GameObjects, which is Steam VR_Behaviour_Pose. The Steam VR_Behaviour_Pose Component essentially takes care of anything related to displaying virtual hands or controllers.

Note that the rig is intelligent enough to know whether or not the controllers are connected, and it will not raise any errors if they are unused. If you do not use the controllers, or you are developing for a platform that does not use them, the Controller GameObjects will not affect performance.

Also note that there is no 3D model of either controller in the scene—SteamVR will grab any controller or hand models at runtime.

Test the Scene

Press the Play button to preview the scene and put on your VR headset.

In the editor, now you can press Play and try out the scene.

Welcome to SteamVR! Yes, it's this easy to get a simple VR demo scene up and running and this is only the beginning! In the next chapter, we will add some interaction to open up that door and go out into the garden! Before that, though, we should take a quick look at the GameObjects that make up the SteamVR rig, what they are and how they can be manipulated.

SteamVR Camera Positioning and Repositioning

Room-scale VR calls for the hardware to track the position of the headset in the room. When you position the [CameraRig] prefab in your Scene, you are in effect setting up the positional link between the real and virtual worlds. The blue rectangle around the camera, which you see in the Unity editor Scene view, represents the default bounds of the play area. You can use the boundaries as a guide to position the real-world room wherever you want in the virtual world (Figure 3.16).

It is possible to move the virtual room area around at runtime. We will look at teleporting in detail in Chapter 6, where we see that it is the entire camera rig that gets repositioned. When a teleport occurs, the entire

FIGURE 3.16 The garden Scene in Unity.

rig moves to the new area, and it is possible to move around in the same physical space, but it then correlates to a different space in the virtual environment.

If you intend to move the user, such as having them moving around inside a vehicle like a car or spaceship, you will need to change the tracking configuration. By default, tracking is set to allow the user to move around the space with the Chaperone system displaying boundaries when the player gets too close to the edges of the play area. With seated experiences (such as those inside vehicles), we need to turn off the boundaries and change the tracking configuration so that our camera no longer acts like a person in a room and more like a person in a static position. We will be looking at this in detail in Chapter 11.

Unless you are setting the vertical position of the player in your own code, when you place the camera rig the blue graphics showing the virtual room boundaries need to be positioned at the correct vertical height so that the bottom of the play area aligns with the ground level in your virtual environment. One common mistake is misaligned floor levels leading to objects positioned lower down than the physical space will allow. This becomes especially important when you are using motion controllers to pick up objects from the ground. If the virtual ground is positioned too high, the user may not be able to grab objects or, worse still, may end up hitting controllers against the floor in the real world. We always need to be extra careful about putting our users in situations that may lead to equipment damage, so keep an eye on your floor levels.

SAVE THE PROJECT AND KEEP BACKUPS!

If you do not already save too often, saving your project is something you need to get used to doing regularly. Very regularly. Because crashes happen, especially with new or cutting-edge technologies like VR. The best way to avoid losing your work is to save regularly and make regular backups of your projects. Seriously, I know backing up can be a real chore, but it is the best way you can spend 5 or 10 minutes of your day. Hard drives do not live forever, and backups may be our only hope. Consider a source control system such as Github, which acts as a remote server to store all your source files safely.

Save the scene with File > Save Scene.

Unity will ask for a name. Call it "garden" and click OK.

Now, save the project. File > Save Project.

PROBLEMS?

Over time, the SteamVR library can change. For example, some readers of the first edition of this book found that the example files no longer worked after SteamVR 2.0 launched. VR moves at a rapid rate. Although I have tried to make it easy to update SteamVR in the example projects, you may have to do some work to update them if the SDK changes in a significant way.

If you have any trouble running example projects for this book in Unity, make sure that you have downloaded the latest version of the projects from the website and check that they have the latest version of the SteamVR SDK inside them. Unity should automatically upgrade older projects to maintain backward compatibility, but SteamVR files and objects may need to be updated manually.

I have tried to future-proof the example files as much as possible by avoiding changing SteamVR specific objects and keeping them "fresh" from the source prefabs. As we rarely change anything on the SteamVR [CameraRig] or Player prefabs themselves, if you have trouble with newer versions of SteamVR (after version 2.0), replace the SteamVR prefabs inside your Scenes—such as the [CameraRig] prefabs or Player prefabs—with new ones from the SteamVR folders and see if that fixes the problem. At the time of writing, SteamVR is at version 2.3.2.

Hopefully you will have no issues with it, but I wanted to make sure you have this information just in case that changes in the future.

RECAP

In this chapter, we took a crash course in the Unity editor by looking at its views and panels. We defined some common terms before diving into a Unity project and downloading the SteamVR library from the Unity Asset Store. The project was set up to be VR-ready and, if all went well, you should have taken the first steps into your own virtual world.

It is time to open the door to the next chapter or, rather, it's time to open a virtual door in the next chapter! Next up, we will look at adding interactivity. To facilitate this, we will use the SteamVR Interaction system.

CHAPTER 4

The SteamVR Interaction System

IN THIS CHAPTER, WE LOOK AT THE Steam virtual reality (SteamVR) interaction system and find out how it can rapidly increase development time by supplying mechanisms for common VR interactions. The SteamVR interaction system is the same one seen in the Valve VR title The Lab, which includes a whole bunch of code to interact with switches, pick up and drop objects, teleportation, and more.

Version 2.0 of the SteamVR library brought with it an overhaul of the input system and input handling. The thoughtful folks at Valve also decided to provide us with a whole lot of code to easily handle most of the day-to-day interactions we might need for VR. Adding teleportation, for example, is a matter of dragging two prefabs into the scene and then choosing which areas can be used by the teleporter. Picking up and dropping objects is also massively simplified and can be accomplished by using just a couple of Components. In this chapter, we will look at adding a method to open a door and add the functionality to be able to teleport around, out of a little house and into the garden.

DOWNLOAD AND EXTRACT EXAMPLE PROJECT SOURCE FILES

If you have not already extracted the example files into a folder on your hard drive, extract them somewhere where you can easily access them. Open the example project for Chapter 4 in Unity and open the main_ scene scene from the Assets folder.

THE PLAYER PREFAB

In the last chapter, we used the CameraRig prefab to add VR to the Scene. For this chapter, we use a different prefab—a camera rig that has a camera, controller/hands, and basic body and object colliders ready to use.

With the main_scene open in Unity, look to the Project browser and find SteamVR > Interaction > Core > Prefabs.

In the Prefabs folder, find the Player prefab (Figure 4.1) and drag it over into the Hierarchy to add it to the current Scene. It should appear just in the right place, inside the little house. If that is not the case, click on Player in the Hierarchy and set all its position and rotation values in the Inspector, to zero.

Make sure that one of your motion-tracked controllers is switched on and press the Play button in Unity to preview the Scene in VR.

Notice that you should have hand(s) gripping the controller (exciting!). The SteamVR Player prefab has hands already configured and ready to use (Figure 4.2).

Now that we have hands, the next step is to make the door interactive so that we can open or close it.

MAKING THE DOOR INTERACTIVE

Although there is no Component to act as a door opener, SteamVR provides several Components do doing things like pulling or pushing objects that will only move in certain ways or rotate around certain axis. One such is the Circular Drive Component. When you try to grab an interactive object that has the Circular Drive Component attached to it,

Setting up an object that can open and close requires two Components:

- **Interactable**

   This Component tells SteamVR that the GameObject is an object that it can interact with.

- **Circular Drive**

   The Circular Drive Component adds the physics, collisions, and events to an object so that it can be grabbed and pulled to rotate around one of its axes. In the case of our door, this will be the Y axis, and we will limit the rotation to between 0° and −90°. That is, the door will be able to open outwards from the house but not inwards.

Click on the Door_Parent GameObject in the Hierarchy.

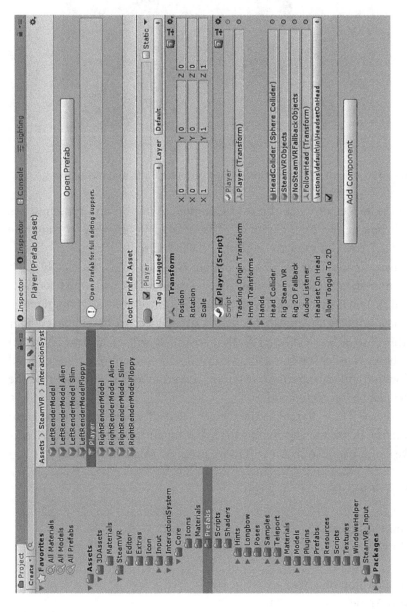

FIGURE 4.1   The SteamVR Player prefab provides basic collision and hands to the VR camera rig.

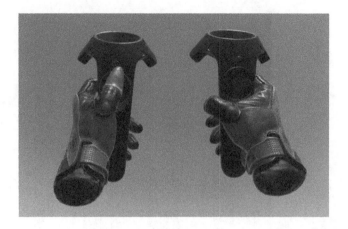

FIGURE 4.2   SteamVR interaction library provides built-in hand support.

In the Inspector, click the Add Component button and type into the search box at the top "Circular." That should be enough to show the Circular Drive Component (Figure 4.3). Click Circular Drive.

When the Circular Drive Component is added to the GameObject, it will automatically add an Interactable Component for you, which as mentioned earlier, is used to deal with the actual controller–object interaction.

I have already arranged the door GameObject to include a collider (in this case, a Box Collider) so that SteamVR will be able to tell when your hand is touching the door. SteamVR's Interactable Component will deal with highlighting the object, too, so it is obvious to the user that the object can be interacted with.

With the Door_Parent GameObject selected in the Hierarchy, head over to the Inspector and change the following properties on that Circular Drive Component so that it will move properly when you grab it:

Axis of Rotation   Y Axis

Limited Rotation
· Limited   CHECKED

Limited Rotation Min
Min Angle   −90

Limited Rotation Max
Max Angle   0

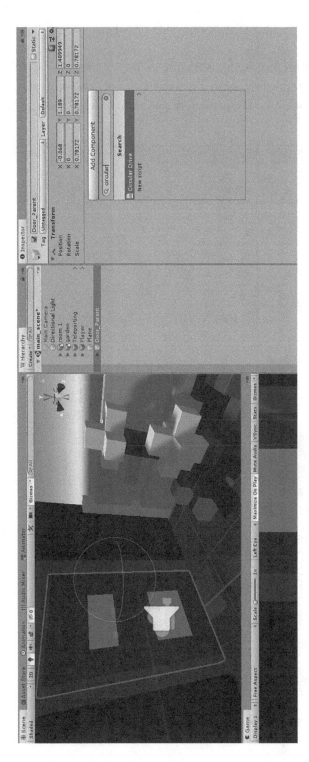

FIGURE 4.3 The Circular Drive Component can be found by typing "circular" into the Add Component search bar.

Now that the Circular Drive Component has been set up, click Play to try it out.

If you can reach it without leaving your play area, you should be able to walk over to the door, grab it (using the trigger on your controller), and push it open or closed (Figure 4.4). If you want to test it but you can't reach

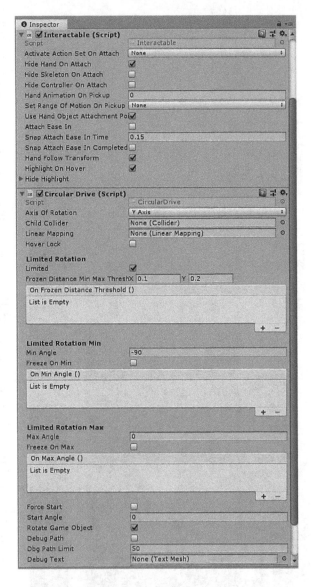

FIGURE 4.4 The door uses SteamVR's Interactable and Circular Drive Components for opening and closing with the controllers.

the doorway without moving, feel free to move the Player GameObject closer to the door (in the Hierarchy or Scene panes).

If you don't have the physical space to walk over to the door, the next section will help. We are now going to set up teleportation so that you can not only open the door but also go through it and out into the garden.

ADD TELEPORTATION

Look to the Project browser window and find SteamVR > Interaction > Teleport > Prefabs.

Inside that Prefabs folder, find the Teleporting prefab and drag it over into the Hierarchy to add it to the Scene (Figure 4.5).

Click on the Teleporting GameObject you just added to the Scene and check out the Teleport Component in the Inspector. From the sound it makes when to teleport to the colors of the pointers and highlights, it is very customizable! The default settings are all we need for now, though.

Below the Teleport Component, there is a Teleport Arc Component. This, again, is a highly customizable Component that will display that nice arc out from the controller to the potential teleportation destination.

The Components are set up already and the default values will do just fine, but feel free to play around and adjust colors.

Next, we need to set up the areas that can be teleported to. We could just make a giant 3D plane and let them teleport wherever they want, but we do not want players to be able to teleport anywhere and potentially end up outside of the boundaries of our world or on top of something they are not supposed to be on top of.

SteamVR teleportation can use two different methods for teleport targeting; we can apply teleportation to a flat plane (or ground model) that will allow players to point anywhere on its surface and teleport freely around. Alternatively, we can use specific locked points for players to move to. They can only move to that specifically defined point.

For this example, we use the flat plane method. I have already added a GameObject called Plane to the Scene.

Find Teleport_Plane in the Hierarchy and click on it to highlight it.

In the Inspector, click the Add Component button. In the search box, type Teleport Area (Figure 4.6). Choose the Teleport Area Component from the list, to add it to the Teleport Plane GameObject.

As soon as the Teleport Area Component is added to Teleport_Plane, the texture of the plane will be automatically replaced by SteamVR's teleport area texture (Figure 4.7). An important note here is that the surface

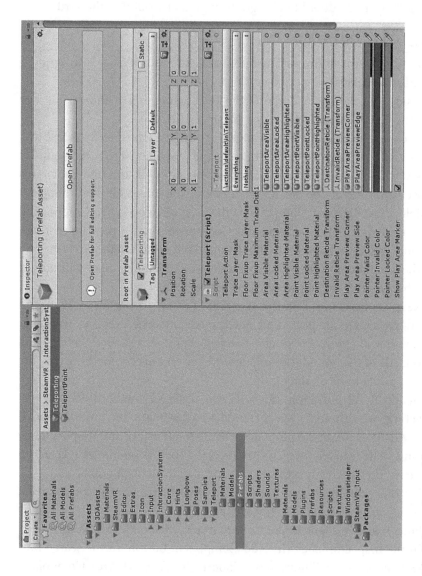

FIGURE 4.5   The Teleporting prefab.

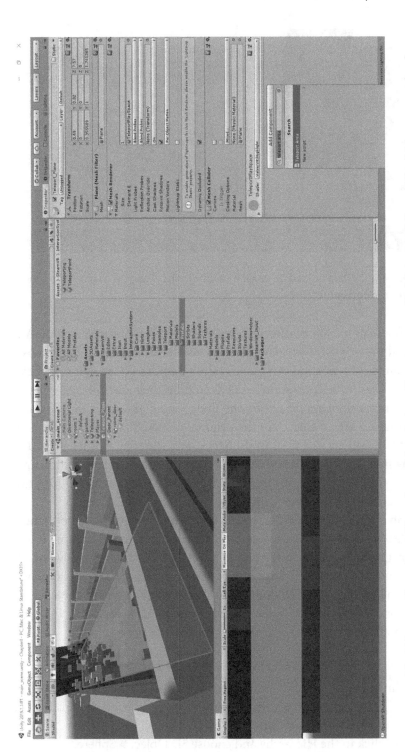

FIGURE 4.6   The Teleport_Plane GameObject has a Teleport Area Component applied to it, to tell SteamVR which areas can be chosen for teleportation.

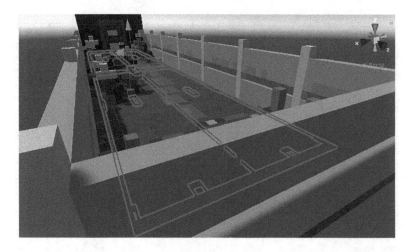

FIGURE 4.7 When added to a GameObject, the Teleport Area Component replaces the current texture.

you choose as a teleportation area will be used as a display inside the VR sim and the original texture will not be visible. This means if you choose, for example, an existing mesh of a room's floor, the floor will disappear. For this reason, teleportation areas should be their own objects—if you were using a floor model, clone the floor model and use the clone as a teleportation area rather than the original object. That way, the original object will still act as a floor in the Scene, and the SteamVR teleportation area will be shown as an addition. Also note that your teleportation area needs a collider of some description on it so that the teleporter script can collide and find the target point being pointed at by the user.

Grab your headset and controllers and give that a go. You should now be able to teleport around, by pressing the trackpad (in VR, SteamVR will automatically overlay a nifty tooltip over the controller to show which button needs to be pressed to teleport). You can now go to the door, open it up, and go outside! Well done! I would say that is a pretty big achievement for a single chapter, but we are not done yet. I say we add something to throw around in here.

PICKING UP AND THROWING OBJECTS

Let's throw things around! In this section, we will make a sphere object and add a Component that will allow us to use the controllers to pick it up, drop it, or simply throw it away!

Right click in the Hierarchy and choose 3D Object > Sphere.

Now select the new sphere in the Hierarchy. Drag it into a place where you will be able to pick it up in VR. For example, I used the position:

X: 0.75

Y: 0.78

Z: 3.9

The coordinates above place the sphere in the garden, not too far outside of the doorway.

As mentioned earlier, all objects utilizing the Interactable Component need a collider to tell when the controllers are trying to interact with them. Unity primitives, like the sphere, already have a collider attached so there is no additional work to do there. Instead, we can just go ahead and add the Throwable Component.

In the Inspector pane, click on the Add Component button.

Start typing into the search box "Throwable" and the SteamVR_ Throwable Component should appear (Figure 4.8). Add SteamVR_ Throwable to the sphere and you're done! Unity will also automatically add any other Components that the Throwable Component relies on.

Once such Component that the Throwable Component uses is the Velocity Estimator. In Chapter 1, in the "Get Your Main Interactions in Place Early" section, I mentioned that for reliable throwing you need to average out the controller velocities rather than just taking a velocity value from the controller. The Velocity Estimator does that for you here. The default value for Velocity Average Frames is 5. This tells the Component to average out the velocity over 5 frame updates, which produces a reliable velocity value based on the speed that the controllers are moving (calculated by the distance moved between frames not the controller's velocity value). This Component also has a separate value for angular velocity, which by default uses 11 frames to calculate the average from rather than the velocity's 5. Take care when modifying these values, as its impact may not be apparent on the controller you are testing with. If you do change these values, I would recommend testing on all the motion controllers you can get your hands on—just to make sure that the throwing effect works the same across them all. Otherwise, leave the values at their defaults and you should get along fine.

Press Play in the editor to preview the scene, and you should now be able to pick up the object and throw it around. Use the trigger to grab the sphere or let go of it.

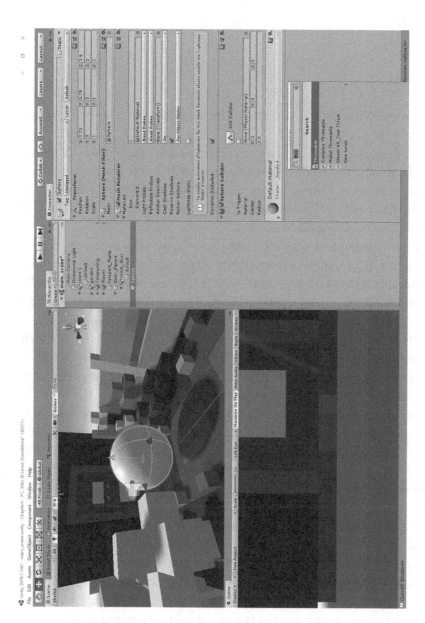

FIGURE 4.8   The Throwable Component allows any physics-based Unity object to be picked up and dropped by the user.

Go ahead and create more spheres to throw around (just repeat the steps above) or maybe add some cubes or cylinders too. Just follow those instructions above, to add SteamVR_Throwable to each one, and it will work. As long as it has a collider, you can add the SteamVR_Throwable Component to almost any 3D object in a Scene.

In Chapter 6—"Advanced Interactions," we will be looking at a hand pose system provided by SteamVR that allows us to set up how the hand is posed when it grabs interactable objects like the one(s) you just made.

RECAP

First, we looked at adding the Player prefab to the scene so that it was set up to move around and interact. Then, we made a door that could be opened and closed with the motion controllers in VR. Finally, we went out into the garden to catch some rays (or, cast some rays—that's a programmer joke!) by adding teleportation to the example project. That is quite a lot of progress for one little chapter, isn't it?

In the next chapter, we look at building a main menu system, tapping into the Interactable Component for controller events and actions. We will look at a method provided by SteamVR for fading in and out the user's view, then look at the correct way to load Scenes when using SteamVR.

CHAPTER 5

Building a Main Menu

I N THIS CHAPTER, WE LOOK AT HOW TO BUILD A MAIN MENU SCENE. AS well as building the user interface (UI), we look at three methods for interacting with UI in virtual reality (VR) and scripting the behaviors to correctly load another Scene when the Start Game button is activated.

UI, for VR, is a new art that we are only just beginning to understand. Old methods of flat screens with buttons feel unnatural in a virtual world, forced in there through necessity rather than to enhance an experience. Some of the best VR interfaces are the ones that act as a part of the universe they inhabit. If an interface has rules that tie into the virtual universe and make sense, it can be much more natural to use.

For example, the game Axe Throw VR by PsychicParrot Games (Figure 5.1) has a menu that gets the players into the action right from the very moment the loading completes. Rather than showing a regular menu screen, there is a conveyor of targets—each representing a menu option— and players must throw axes at the targets to choose items. Not only does this make for a more interesting and fun main menu, but it also teaches the player how to play the game right away and without them even realizing it. To be able to start the game, the player must understand how to grab an axe from the backpack, take it out, and throw it at the target—the three skills required to play the game itself. To help them to do this, icons are shown in the environment. The icons can be understood either with or without text, meaning that most players do not even need to read to be able to pick up these new mechanics.

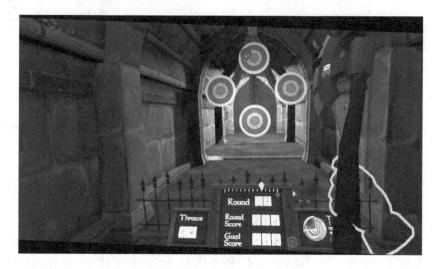

FIGURE 5.1   The menu of Axe Throw VR by PsychicParrot Games teaches players the games' basic mechanics before the game even starts.

By the time players get to the main axe throwing game, they already know what to expect when an axe is thrown. Not just in the basic actions required to get an axe and throw it, but also how the axe will fly toward the targets. The game's learning process is built right into the menu from the start. The menu acts as both a tutorial and a fun way to navigate the various available game modes and settings.

"SHOW, DON'T TELL!"

When it comes to VR design, I live by three words—"Show, don't tell." That is, be as visual and interactive as you can be. In VR, immersion is helped by your user's feeling as though everything is a part of a virtual universe with comprehendible and consistent rules and behaviors. Part of the fun for users is figuring out how things behave in those worlds, of interacting with them and playing. If your interfaces can be a part of the universe you are creating, it is going to make for a much more enjoyable experience for your users.

That said, there is a necessity sometimes to use regular UI elements such as those provided by Unity Graphical UI (GUI). For that reason, we will start this chapter by looking at ways to work with Unity's UI system. After that, we will look at making SteamVR physics-based buttons that your users will be able to press down with the controllers.

BUILDING THE MAIN MENU UI WITH UNITY GUI

Unity GUI draws interface elements to something called a Canvas. It's just like it sounds—a Canvas is a virtual surface for drawing graphics and text onto. Unity Canvases can be drawn in two different ways; Either direct to the screen in Screen Space—locked to the camera—or to World Space, whereby the Canvas acts as a 3D object (similar to a plane) that you can move around, rotate, and scale and so forth.

In order to work as a VR interface, we render the Canvas in World Space. This is just a setting you can choose on the Canvas Component. When rendered in World Space, we can position the Canvas in the 3D environment just like a regular 3D object, position the Canvas anywhere and potentially walk around it.

Unity GUI

Essentially, anything that you can make with the regular Unity GUI system is up for grabs in VR. The system we will be using here will just hook into Unity's existing systems to do the actual UI work, leaving SteamVR to deal with detecting when the controller is trying to interact by using scripts provided as part of the SteamVR library.

Open the Example Project

In Unity, open the example project for this chapter. In the Project browser, find the main_menu_1 Scene and double click to open it up.

In the Scene, you will see a basic UI—made using only buttons—drawn on a Canvas that is rendered in World Space, located on the side of a cube in the 3D environment.

By default, the built-in UI behaviors have nothing to do with motion-tracked VR controllers. Trying to click or push a Unity GUI button in VR, for example, would have no effect at all. Unity GUI does provide a method for interaction with a 2D interface, but we need to use SteamVR Components and a Collider, to make our UI elements work with the controller.

GETTING STEAMVR TO WORK WITH YOUR UI

Next, we add the Components required for SteamVR support.

In the Hierarchy, find and expand out the MenuCanvas GameObject by clicking on the little arrow next to it. You should see

MenuCanvas

Start_Button

Exit_Button

Title

Click on Start_Button. In the Inspector, click Add Component.

At the top of the Component menu, type UI Element into the search box. Choose UI Element from the menu. The UI Element may be thought of as being a bit like a bridge between the Unity GUI system and SteamVR. It connects the two together.

Unity will add the UI Element and automatically add an Interactable Component, too, which has the code we need to detect when a controller is touching or clicking on the UI element. The UI Element script uses Interactable to know what the controller is trying to do, before relaying any interaction to the Unity GUI system, to react to.

Now that the interaction Components are set up, all that is left to do is to add a collider so that the system can detect the controller and button collisions.

Click Add Component again. Type "Box Collider" into the search box and add a Box Collider to the button. By default, the size of the box collider will be wrong, as there is no mesh attached to the button object directly for the collider to get dimensions from. For that reason, we need to set its size properties manually. Use these values for the Box Collider Component:

Size X: 165

Size Y: 33

Size Z: 58

The final Collider should look something like the one in Figure 5.2.

The start button is ready to go, and we can now repeat the same steps to set up the exit button.

In the Hierarchy, click the Exit_Button GameObject.

Go to the Inspector and choose Add Component. Type "UI Element" and add the UI Element Component (and Interactable) to the GameObject.

Finally, click Add Component again and type "Box Collider" into the search box. Add the Box Collider and set its size properties to the same ones as the Start_Button:

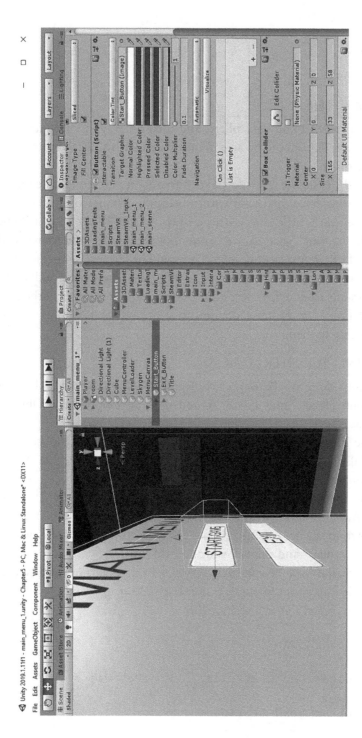

FIGURE 5.2   The Box Collider for the Start_Button GameObject.

Size X: 165

Size Y: 33

Size Z: 58

TEST OUT THE SCENE!

Grab your headset and controllers, and then hit Play in Unity to try out the interface. You should be able to now reach out and click buttons with your controller.

This is the easiest way to use UI with SteamVR, but it might be impractical to always have interfaces within walking distance of the play area. For that reason, a little later in this chapter, in the "Using a Laser Pointer for UI Interaction" section, we bring another way of interacting to the table by offering up a laser pointer. Users will be able to use the pointer to point at the interface (which can be as close or far away as you like) and click elements from a distance, rather than having to be near to them.

Right now, our buttons do nothing. In the next section, we add functionality to them.

REACTING TO INTERACTION

The buttons need to talk to a script. The script Component will be called MenuController.cs, and it will be added to an empty GameObject in the Scene.

In the Hierarchy, right click in an empty space and choose Create Empty (also accessible via the menus at the top of Unity, GameObject > Empty GameObject).

Name the new GameObject "MenuController." In the Inspector, choose Add Component and from the Add Component menu, scroll right down to the bottom and choose "New Script." Name the new script "MenuController" and click Create and Add.

Right click on the new MenuController Component in the Inspector, and choose Edit Script to open up the script editor.

Type this script into the script editor:

```
using UnityEngine;

public class MenuController : MonoBehaviour
{
    public void StartGame()
    {
```

```
        Debug.Log("Start game...");
    }

    public void ExitGame()
    {
        Debug.Log("Exit game...");
        Application.Quit();
    }
}
```

Script Breakdown

The script above starts with a using statement to tell Unity that we want to use the UnityEngine classes (which allow us to close the game and so forth). After the class declaration, there are two main functions:

```
    public void StartGame()
    {
        Debug.Log("Start game...");
    }

    public void ExitGame()
    {
        Debug.Log("Exit game...");
        Application.Quit();
    }
```

The StartGame() function uses Debug.Log to send a message to Unity's debug console, to let us know that the button has been pressed. The ExitGame() will send out a message to say "Exit game..." to the console, followed by exiting the game if it is running outside of Unity.

Also in the ExitGame() function is Application.Quit(), which will shut down the executable whenever it is running as a stand-alone executable outside of the Unity editor. Note that this statement will do nothing when it is called from inside Unity and only works in stand-alone builds.

Now that we have the script in place to react to the button presses, the final step is to hook up the GUI buttons to the script.

Attach Buttons to the Script

In the Hierarchy, find the Start_Button GameObject again (under the MenuCanvas GameObject). Click the Start_Button in the Hierarchy to highlight it. In the Inspector, you may need to scroll down a little to find the UI Element Component you added earlier in this section, so do whatever you need to see UI Element in the Inspector.

The UI Element Component has an On Hand Click (Hand) section (Figure 5.3) that we use to tell the UI what to do whenever this UI element is clicked. Click on the small + icon to add a.

In the empty Component field beneath "Runtime Only," you need to drag and drop in the MenuController GameObject. Once the MenuController GameObject is in the On Hand Click section, click the dropdown to the right of it. Find MenuController in the dropdown menu and highlight it, which should open a second dropdown where you can select functions from inside that MenuController.cs script (Figure 5.4).

Choose StartGame() from the second dropdown menu.

The procedure is the same for the exit button. Find and highlight Exit_ Button in the Hierarchy, then drag and drop the MenuController GameObject into the UI Element's On Hand Click event. Choose MenuController in the dropdown and ExitGame() from the second dropdown.

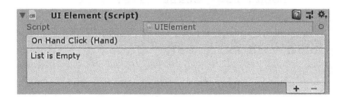

FIGURE 5.3   The UI Element Component allows SteamVR to talk to Unity GUI.

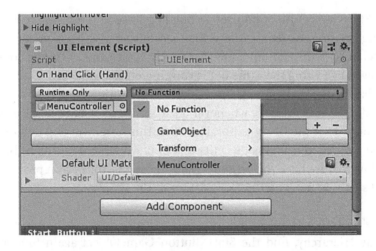

FIGURE 5.4   The UI Element Component can call a function on a GameObject of your choice.

Bring up the Console in Unity by pressing CTRL+SHIFT+C.

Press Play in the editor to try out your interface. When you select a button, you should see a message appear in the Console window to let you know which button has been clicked. If this is the case, we know that everything is working correctly.

To be able to actually start the game whenever the StartGame() function is called, rather than just sending out a debug message to the console, we first need to look at how Unity loads Scenes and how we need to load them differently for VR. In the next section, we will add Scene loading to the menu.

LOADING SCENES CORRECTLY WITH STEAMVR

Unity's regular SceneManager methods work well for desktop loading, but the loading process can often stall the images in the headset with uncomfortable frame rate drops. The SteamVR_LoadLevel class allows us to avoid this by smoothly transitioning from the Unity scene into something called the Steam Compositor. If you are familiar with SteamVR, you may recognize the most frequently seen part of the Compositor as being the landscape with the big Earth in the sky where it says, "This is Real." Essentially, you can think of the Steam Compositor as being a desktop for your VR headset. When you are outside of a VR application, rather than the headset switching off or going to a blank screen, we get to see the Compositor instead. At its most basic level, the Compositor takes care of handing off from one VR application to another but it also serves several other purposes such as drawing Chaperone bounds and other system messages like the current interpupillary distance (IPD) setting when you turn the IPD knob on the side of a Vive. We have some limited access to the Compositor via the SteamVR Unity library to do things like draw a loading progress bar or to display a different surrounding skybox whenever the Compositor takes over the display.

Using SteamVR_LoadLevel, we transition out into the Compositor as Unity loads the Scene and after loading completes, we smoothly fade back into Unity.

As an extra bonus, the SteamVR_LoadLevel Component lets you add your own skybox to display as users are waiting to load. SteamVR not just lets you add a skybox, but also gives you the tools to be able to make your own skybox that looks like the inside of your Unity Scene. We will be looking at SteamVR_Skybox later in the "Making Your Own Skybox Inside Unity" section in this chapter.

Adding Scene Loading to Your Menu

This section will continue where we left off in the previous section (Building a Main Menu Interface). If you intend to follow along with the exercises in the next section, please make sure that you have completed everything in this chapter so far.

Reopen the example project Chapter 5—Project 1 from the examples, then open the Scene named main_menu.

Create a LevelLoader GameObject

Create a new GameObject (GameObject > Empty GameObject) and name it LevelLoader.

With the new LevelLoader GameObject selected, click Add Component in the Inspector and type Load Level into the search bar.

Choose SteamVR_Load Level from the menu. Right now, this will not do anything. We will call it from another script (the MenuController) further in this chapter. Before we do, let's take a look at the SteamVR_ Load Level Component properties to see what can be customized.

The SteamVR_Load Level Component Starting at the top of the Inspector, here is a quick breakdown of what all those parameters are for, on the SteamVR_Load Level Component:

1. **Level Name**

   This is the name of the level that SteamVR_LoadLevel will load when its Trigger() function is called.

2. **Internal Process Path and Internal Process Args**

   These are (according to some) used by Valve for accessing external processes when loading executable files outside of Unity. We do not need to use them for regular SteamVR Scene loading.

3. **Load Additive**

   Should the current Scene be unloaded from memory to make way for the Scene SteamVR is loading, or should this new Scene be loaded "on top" of the current one and combined with it? Additive loading is just that—adding the new Scene to the current one.

4. **Load Async**

   This should remain checked if you intend to use a progress bar (if you don't have this checked your progress bar will never fill). Loading asynchronously should also mean that there is less of a chance of frame rate drops in the headset, during loads.

5. **Progress Bar Empty and Progress Bar Full**
You can provide two images for a progress bar. SteamVR will display them for you. The empty image should be a progress bar with an empty inside (Figure 5.5), and the progress bar full image should be the same image only with the inside filled (Figure 5.6). SteamVR will progressively overlay the full progress bar image on top of the empty image, in an amount between 0 and 100% depending on the state of loading at the time.

6. **Loading Screen Width in Meters and Progress Bar Width in Meters**
Here, you can set the sizes of your loading screen and progress bar. As this is VR, the measurements are in meters rather than generic units as would usually be the case in Unity measurements.

7. **Loading Screen Distance**
How far would you like to see the loading screen from the camera? Enter the number here in meters.

8. **Loading Screen Transform**
As far as I can tell, this is a reference to a Transform used when displaying the loading screen, but it appears to be set up by SteamVR and not something we need to do anything specific with.

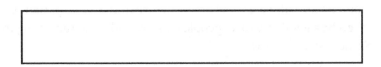

FIGURE 5.5   An empty progress bar image.

FIGURE 5.6   A full progress bar image.

9. **Progress Bar Transform**
   Same as the Loading Screen Transform, this is used by SteamVR and not something we need to do anything with.

10. **Front, Back, Left, Right, Top, and Bottom**
    Rather than showing the default SteamVR skybox (the sky with the planet Earth in) it will show your custom skybox if you drag and drop in textures for a custom skybox. See "Making Your Own Skybox Inside Unity" for a method to create your own skyboxes, further in this chapter.

11. **Background Color**
    You can set a background color here, which is one way to customize the look of loading without having to use a custom skybox.

12. **Show Grid**
    If this is checked, SteamVR will draw the grid during loading.

13. **Fade Out Time**
    How long the fade out should take before moving to the Compositor screen, in seconds.

14. **Fade In Time**
    How long the fade in should be after we return from the Compositor back to the new Unity Scene.

15. **Postload Settle Time**
    After a Scene has loaded, you can allow a little time for the user to acclimatize to the change by adding a little delay here (in seconds). The progress bar will stay on the screen during this delay, and the Compositor will fade it out smoothly when the delay period is over. It can be a good way to let people look around before anything in the Scene becomes active.

16. **Loading Screen Fade In Time and Loading Screen Fade Out Time**
    Fade in and out times for showing the loading screen and/or Compositor environment.

17. **Auto Trigger On Enabled**
    By checking this box, you can have SteamVR activate the loading procedure automatically, as soon as this GameObject is enabled (which happens either when the Scene starts, or a previously disabled GameObject is enabled through another script).

Add Level Loading to the MenuController Script Component

You may remember from the previous section, "Reacting to Interaction," that we left this script hooked up to the buttons but not actually doing anything when they were clicked. In this section, we will react to the start game button and actually load the main game Scene.

Click MenuController in the Hierarchy. In the Inspector, right click the MenuController Component and choose "Edit Script" to open the script editor.

To communicate with SteamVR scripts, we need to add the using statement to the script, which will give access to the Valve.VR namespace.

Below the line:

```
using UnityEngine;
```

Add:

```
using Valve.VR;
```

Now that we can talk to the classes within the Valve.VR namespace (the SteamVR scripts), we want to add a variable that will hold a reference to the level loader Component (SteamVR_LoadLevel) which we added to the LevelLoader GameObject in the previous section.

Below the class declaration:

```
public class MenuController : MonoBehaviour
{
```

Add:

```
public SteamVR_LoadLevel _levelLoader;
```

Do not worry about adding the reference to the level loader right away. Once the script is finished, we can go back to the editor and take care of that. Let's move on, to add the code that will load the main Scene.

In the StartGame() function, below the Debug.Log statement (but before the closing bracket for the function):

```
    public void StartGame()
    {
```

```
        Debug.Log("Start game...");
```

Add:

```
        // now tell SteamVR to load the main game
scene
        _levelLoader.levelName = "main_scene";
        _levelLoader.fadeOutTime = 1f;
        _levelLoader.Trigger();
```

The completed script should now look like this:

```
using UnityEngine;
using Valve.VR;

public class MenuController : MonoBehaviour
{
     public SteamVR_LoadLevel _levelLoader;

   public void StartGame()
   {
        Debug.Log("Start game...");

        // now tell SteamVR to load the main game
scene
        _levelLoader.levelName = "main_scene";
        _levelLoader.fadeOutTime = 1f;
        _levelLoader.Trigger();
   }

   public void ExitGame()
   {
        Debug.Log("Exit game...");
        Application.Quit();
   }
}
```

Script Breakdown   First up, there's the line at the top to allow us to talk to SteamVR:

```
using UnityEngine;
using Valve.VR;
```

Just below the class declaration, we declare the variable _levelLoader:

```
public class MenuController : MonoBehaviour
{
        public SteamVR_LoadLevel _levelLoader;
```

The Start() function also had some extra code:

```
        // now tell SteamVR to load the main game
scene
        _levelLoader.levelName = "main_scene";
        _levelLoader.fadeOutTime = 1f;
        _levelLoader.Trigger();
```

To have the level loader script do its thing and load in a new Scene, it requires the levelName to be set. This is just a string containing the name of the Scene you would like it to load. Above, I also set the fadeOutTime of the levelLoader so that our VR sim will have a nice 1 second fade out before loading (and a 1 second fade in again when the new Scene is ready).

To tell the levelLoader to load, we call its Trigger() function.

With the code ready to go, you will just need to set up the SteamVR_ Load Level reference on the MenuController Component. Save your script and head back to the Unity editor.

Set Up the Level Loader Reference

In the Hierarchy (in the editor), click on the MenuController GameObject to highlight it and show its properties in the Inspector.

With the MenuController still selected, find the LevelLoader GameObject in the Hierarchy, then click and drag LevelLoader out of the Hierarchy and into the Inspector, into the field named Level Loader.

The reference to Level Loader is now set up and ready to go. Your script MenuController can now make the call to load the level, but it will not work until the Scenes have been added to Unity's Build Settings.

Add Scenes to Build Settings

In Unity, select the menus File > Build Settings.

Unity's Build Settings needs to know which Scenes to include in a build, otherwise Unity will show an error whenever you try to load them. We need to add all Scenes to the "Scenes In Build" section of Build Settings.

Make sure that both the main_menu and main_scene Scenes are in the Build Settings "Scenes In Build" list. Whenever you want to move between Scenes and load different Scenes, they will need to be in the Build Settings to work.

Test Level Loading

Everything should now be in place for loading the level from the main menu. Grab your headset and controllers and press Play in the editor to try it out. Click Start Game and it should go to the main_scene garden.

In the next section, we look at an alternative input method that will allow you to put your UI windows wherever you like in the virtual world—the laser pointer.

USING A LASER POINTER FOR UI INTERACTIONS (AND AN INTRODUCTION TO SCRIPTING WITH THE STEAMVR INPUT SYSTEM)

Rather than having to reach out and physically touch buttons with the controllers, another common method of interaction for VR is to use a laser pointer. This is where a laser pointer emits from the top of the controller (Vive wand, etc.) and users point at whichever button or interface element they want to interact with. A UI element can be activated using one of the buttons, or the trigger, on the controller. SteamVR does include a Component that acts as a laser pointer, but we will need to do a little scripting to get it to communicate with the UI system.

Scripting the action of clicking on a UI element also serves as a great place to start with the SteamVR input system, the actions system, and how we can program a script to know when the user is trying to do something with the controller.

Add Components to the Hands GameObjects

Open the example project for this chapter again, if it is not still open from the previous section. The project name is Chapter 5—Project 1.

In the Hierarchy, find the Player GameObject and expand it out so that you can see what it contains. It should be something along the lines of:

SteamVRObjects

NoSteamVRFallbackObjects (this one may be disabled)

FollowHead

InputModule

PlayVolume (this may be disabled)

DebugUI

Expand out the SteamVRObjects GameObject to show what it contains. Should be something like:

BodyCollider

LeftHand

RightHand

VRCamera

Overlay (may be grayed out / disabled)

[SteamVR]

In the Hierarchy, click on the GameObject named LeftHand, then hold down the SHIFT key on the keyboard and click RightHand so that both LeftHand and RightHand are selected at the same time.

In the Inspector, click on Add Component. In the Search bar at the top of the Add Component window, type Laser and the SteamVR_Laser Pointer Component should show up. If not, you may have to type the full "Steam VR_Laser Pointer" for it to appear.

Click on SteamVR_Laser Pointer in the search results to add it to the LeftHand and RightHand GameObjects.

You now have a laser pointer set up for both controllers. Next, we will set it up to do something when you select the interface.

Add Controller Input to the Laser Pointer

With LeftHand and RightHand GameObjects still selected, click Add Component in the Inspector and choose New Script.

Name the new script "LaserButtonClicker" and click Create and Add. The new empty Component should now appear as a Component in the Inspector. Double click the Script field, or right click the Laser Button Clicker Component and choose Edit Script.

As this is a new script, Unity will have added its template text. Replace that entire script with the following:

```
using System.Collections;
using System.Collections.Generic;
using UnityEngine;
using UnityEngine.UI;

using Valve.VR;
using Valve.VR.Extras;
using Valve.VR.InteractionSystem;

public class LaserButtonClicker : MonoBehaviour
{
    public SteamVR_Input_Sources myHand;
    public SteamVR_Action_Boolean interactAction =
SteamVR_Input.GetAction<SteamVR_Action_Boolean>("defau
lt","InteractUI");

    private SteamVR_LaserPointer laserPointer;
    private GameObject btn;

    private bool pointerOnButton = false;

    void Start()
    {
        laserPointer =
GetComponent<SteamVR_LaserPointer>();

        laserPointer.PointerIn +=
LaserPointer_PointerIn;
        laserPointer.PointerOut +=
LaserPointer_PointerOut;
    }

    private void LaserPointer_PointerIn(object
sender, PointerEventArgs e)
    {
        if (e.target.gameObject.
GetComponent<Button>() != null && btn == null)
        {
            btn = e.target.gameObject;
            InputModule.instance.
HoverBegin(btn);
```

```
                pointerOnButton = true;
        }
    }

    private void LaserPointer_PointerOut(object
sender, PointerEventArgs e)
    {
        if (btn != null)
        {
            pointerOnButton = false;
            InputModule.instance.HoverEnd(btn);
            btn = null;
        }
    }

    void Update()
    {
        if (pointerOnButton)
        {
            if(interactAction[myHand].stateDown)
            {
                InputModule.instance.
Submit(btn);
            }
        }
    }
}
```

Go back to the Unity editor. In the Inspector you should see some new fields on the Laser Button Clicker Component. Those are:

My Hand

Interact Action

These fields will be automatically populated with dropdown menus, due to their types.

Script Breakdown
The LaserButtonClicker.cs script starts with:

```
using System.Collections;
using System.Collections.Generic;
```

```
using UnityEngine;
using UnityEngine.UI;
```

We start out with Unity's standard libraries (System.Collections, System. Collections.Generic, and UnityEngine) then there is an added UnityEngine. UI, which allows our script to access Unity UI classes like Button (which we use later on in the script).

Next, there are three libraries we need for SteamVR. Those are

```
using Valve.VR;
using Valve.VR.Extras;
using Valve.VR.InteractionSystem;
```

To be able to access anything to do with SteamVR via script, you will need Valve.VR libraries. Within those, however, are some extra bits we need for this. Valve.VR.Extras gives us, amongst other things, access to the SteamVR_LaserPointer class. We will need this further on in the script.

Finally in those using statements is the Valve.VR.InteractionSystem. We need this to be able to access the scripts that make up the SteamVR Interaction system.

With using statements out of the way, let's move on to the variable declarations:

```
public SteamVR_Input_Sources myHand;
```

If you are familiar with previous versions of SteamVR, it used to be the case that you needed to talk to the SteamVR_TrackedObject and SteamVR_Controller Components to directly find out what the controllers were doing. In SteamVR 2.x, controllers have been separated out by the new input system. Rather than dealing with controller input (buttons and triggers and so forth) directly, we deal with actions instead. To get to actions, we go via SteamVR's class called Hands.

myHand is declared as being of type SteamVR_Input_Sources. SteamVR_Input_Sources is an enumerated type consisting of a list intended to categorize the object involved in an interaction. It has values like LeftHand, RightHand, Any, LeftFoot, RightFoot, and can be used to identify several different input types such as Vive Trackers, controllers, gamepads, and other tracking devices. For this example, we specify which hand we would like to use to activate the laser pointer, and the value of myHand can be set in the Inspector window inside the Unity editor. We will use the value of myHand to check for actions further on in the script.

In the next line, we see

```
public SteamVR_Action_Boolean
interactAction = SteamVR_Input.GetAction<SteamVR_
Action_Boolean>("default","InteractUI");
```

interactAction is a reference to the action that we will be looking for to act as a "click" on the UI. In this case, we use the "InteractUI" action from the "default" action set. Remember when we first ran a project with SteamVR in it (back in Chapter 3: Creating a New Unity Project) and we had to set up and generate actions via the SteamVR Input window? The actions here refer directly to those actions from SteamVR Input.

In Unity, go to the Window menu and choose SteamVR Input to bring up the SteamVR Input window.

Near the top of the window, under Action Sets, you can see all the default action sets. Those are default (this will probably be only one appearing in an editable text field—that's there to show you which one is currently selected and to allow you to change its name, if needed), platformer, buggy, mixedreality.

Under the Action Sets section is a list of Actions. Find and click on InteractUI to bring up its properties (Figure 5.7). There is a Type, which can be Boolean, Vector1,2 or 3, pose, or skeleton. For something like a button or a trigger you will always use Boolean (which can only have a state of either of or on/0 or 1). There are a few other properties, but we do not need to worry about those just yet.

At the bottom of the window are two buttons: Save and generate and Open binding UI.

Click on the Open binding UI button. If Unity asks if you would like to Save, click yes and let it save. A browser window should open outside Unity (Figure 5.8) showing any active controllers.

Under the "Current Binding" section, you should see whichever type of controller you have currently switched on and plugged in, with an Edit button. If no controllers are attached, you may see a Default binding.

Click Edit, to bring up the controller bindings screen (Figure 5.9).

Along the top of the page are tabs that match up with those Action Sets we saw earlier inside Unity—the ones from the SteamVR Input window: default, platformer, buggy, and mixedreality. The selected one should be "default"—but if it is not—click the default tab to make it so.

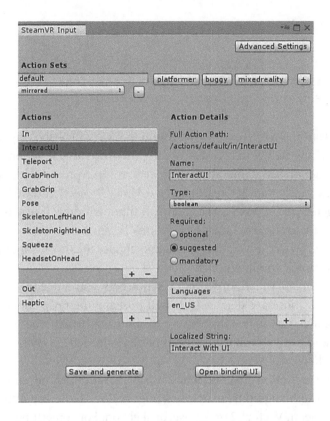

FIGURE 5.7 The SteamVR Input window allows you to set up actions for interactions.

FIGURE 5.8 The Controller Bindings browser page.

On the left side of the page is a list of inputs for the left controller: System, Trigger, Trackpad, Thumb Stick, and buttons.

Click the + icon to the right of the word Trigger and you should see that the action assigned to Click is Interact With UI. So, what you are looking at here is the action named InteractUI being bound to the click event of

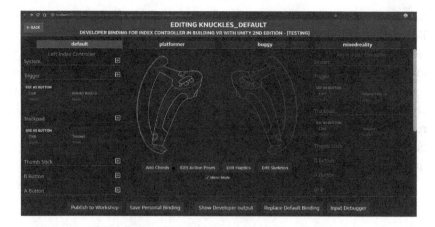

FIGURE 5.9   The Controller Bindings for a specific controller.

the trigger. From this browser-based binding interface, you can rebind all the actions to any input you like. For now, leave them as is. The important thing is that you see the relationship between the controller buttons, bindings, and how they apply back to actions in Unity. We will never directly reference the trigger on the controller. Instead, we reference the action of InteractUI and let SteamVR use its bindings system to figure out when the user is trying to interact, and we let the bindings system deal with any direct input from the controllers, such as the trigger or button presses.

The beauty of this system is that people can bind any controller to your game via Steam, and most controllers will automatically work "out of the box," thanks to the work of the SteamVR team and its automatic binding of common inputs and controllers.

With this background knowledge in place, let's return to the laser pointer script:

```
private SteamVR_LaserPointer laserPointer;
private GameObject btn;

private bool pointerOnButton = false;
```

We will need a reference to the laser pointer script to be able to find out what it is the user is pointing at, so we add the variable for this above, called laserPointer.

Next is a variable called btn that will store the current UI button being pointed at by the laserPointer (null if it is not being pointed at a button)—we will detect the object being pointed at, further down in the main part of the script. Finally, in our variable declarations, we have a Boolean variable named pointerOnButton, used to act as a quick way to keep tabs on whether the pointer is pointing at a button. We need to know this because the pointer does not differentiate the objects it registers. The pointer looks for any Collider. Further down in the script, we will check what type of object the Collider is attached to and store the resulting Boolean value in this variable. After that, we can check against pointerOnButton before trying to do anything button related that might otherwise cause an error.

```
    void Start()
    {
            laserPointer = GetComponent<SteamVR_
LaserPointer>();
            laserPointer.PointerIn += LaserPointer_
PointerIn;
            laserPointer.PointerOut += LaserPointer_
PointerOut;
    }
```

In the Start() function above, laserPointer is set as a reference to the SteamVR_LaserPointer Component attached to the same GameObject by using Unity's built-in GetComponent(). Once we have a reference to the laserPointer class, we can subscribe to its events PointerIn and PointerOut.

If you have never dealt with events in Unity, essentially you start with the event (from the script you are subscribing to) followed by either += to subscribe to it, or −= to unsubscribe. You then add the name of the function in your own script that you want it to call when the event is triggered.

The PointerIn event will be fired inside the SteamVR_LaserPointer class whenever the laser pointer hits an applicable collider. The PointerOut event is fired when it leaves the collider.

In the code above, we subscribe so that when the pointer enters a state where it is "in" a collider, our function LaserPointer_PointerIn() will be called. Whenever the pointer leaves and moves "out" of a collider, our function LaserPointer_PointerOut() will be called.

```
    private void LaserPointer_PointerIn(object
sender, PointerEventArgs e)
    {
```

Our function LaserPointer_PointerIn() will be used to try to discover what it is the pointer is pointing at and, if it's a button, to start a mouseover event. Note LaserPointer_PointerIn() needs two parameters to be passed in; an object called sender, which will give us a reference to the instance of the class calling this function, followed by PointerEventArgs (e), which contains information about what the pointer is currently pointing at. These parameters are passed in from the SteamVR_LaserPointer class whenever the PointerIn or PointerOut events are triggered and have we use PointerEventArgs to get the GameObject that the pointer is pointing to

```
        if (e.target.gameObject.GetComponent
<Button>() != null && btn == null)
          {
```

One of the arguments passed in is called target. By checking to see if a Component named Button is attached to the target GameObject, we know whether the object is a button and therefore a valid target for us to interact with. The statement above also checks that btn is null, which is there to make sure that any previous reference we have to a button is cleared out (which happens in the LaserPointer_PointerOut() function below) before we risk overwriting it with a new reference before ending the interaction with the previous one.

   If those conditions are met, we know that we have a button and we can go ahead now and get a reference to it, start an interaction and set our pointerOnButton bool to true:

```
              btn = e.target.gameObject;
              InputModule.instance.
HoverBegin(btn);
              pointerOnButton = true;
```

In an earlier section of this chapter, "Getting SteamVR to Work with Your UI," we made it so that the controller would work with the buttons whenever the controller was inside the button's Box Collider. SteamVR uses a class called InputModule to make this happen. It tells Unity UI when we are trying to interact with UI. InputModule is a Singleton, by the way, which means there will only ever be one instance of it in memory at any time, and we can access it by using InputModule.instance.

Here in the script above, we bypass the regular method for controller collision by telling the InputModule directly to interact with the button we are pointing at. We are telling the InputModule to start doing whatever it does when we would normally hover over a button—by calling HoverBegin()—and then we pass in a reference to the GameObject of the button that the laser pointer is pointing to, as passed in to this script via those PointerEventArgs in the variable e, and stored in the variable btn at the start of the function.

Calling InputModule is a quick way to force things to happen with UI elements, such as activating them or forcing them to highlight.

The next part of the script deals with what happens when the laser pointer is not pointing at a GameObject:

```
    private void LaserPointer_PointerOut(object
sender, PointerEventArgs e)
    {
        if (btn != null)
        {
            pointerOnButton = false;
            InputModule.instance.HoverEnd(btn);
            btn = null;
        }
    }
```

LaserPointer_PointerOut() will be called whenever the laser pointer leaves a collider, so in the above case, we want to send a message to the InputModule instance to end the button's highlighted state. To do this, we call HoverEnd() and pass in a reference to the GameObject of the button we want to stop "hovering over." The HoverEnd() function takes care of dehighlighting the button for us.

Finally, we clear out the reference in the btn variable, and we are ready to start a new interaction whenever the laser pointer hits another UI element.

That is how we can make the laser pointer work with a UI. I think you will agree that using InputModule for forcing UI events is a useful little tool to have!

BUILDING THE MAIN MENU UI WITH STEAMVR PHYSICAL BUTTONS

As mentioned at the start of this chapter, in VR you should always follow my golden rule:

Show, don't tell.

Here, we build a button using the SteamVR Hover Button Component. This is a great way to make pressable physical buttons with minimal work.

Open the Example Project

Open the example project for this chapter, Chapter 5—Project 2. In the Assets folder, find and open the main_menu Scene.

Build a Physics-Based Button

In the Hierarchy, there is an empty GameObject named Start Button. Click on the Start Button GameObject to highlight it.

The button has the following structure:

> Start Button: An empty GameObject with the required Components attached.
> > Button Model: A scaled 3D cube that will act as the physical button. Also has a Box Collider Component attached to it.
> > > MenuCanvas: A Unity GUI Canvas for rendering text.
> > > > Start_Game: A text object to display the words START GAME.

We will be using this Start Button for this section, but it is expected that you will replace the Button Model GameObject (which is a simple 3D cube) with your own custom 3D button models when you build out your own interfaces.

Add SteamVR Button Components

SteamVR provides everything we need in terms of scripting the physics-based button. We just need to add a single Component to the button and Unity will do most of the work for us.

Click the Start Button GameObject in the Hierarchy, to highlight it.

In the Inspector, click Add Component. In the search box, type Hover button. From the list, find the Hover Button Component and add it to your GameObject. Unity will add this and the Interactable Component too, which the Hover Button Component will use to deal with its relationship to the controllers.

Hook Up the Button to Scripting

With the Start Button GameObject selected, we find the events in the Inspector. They are shown in lighter gray areas with the headings On Button Down (Hand), On Button Up (Hand) and On Button Is Pressed (Hand).

In the On Button Down (Hand) event, click the plus button (Figure 5.10).

In the Hierarchy, grab the MenuController GameObject and drag it over into that On Button Down (Hand) event in the field below the Runtime Only dropdown. This tells the Component that we want to call a script on our MenuController GameObject when the On Button Down event is fired.

The dropdown on the right side of that On Button Down event should now be available to select any scripts attached to the MenuController. Click on the dropdown and choose MenuController > StartGame.

In that Hover Button Component, the final setting is to tell SteamVR how much to allow our button to move when we press it. Find Local Move Distance and use the following numbers:

X: 0

Y: −0.05

Z: 0

Test the Scene

Grab your headset and controller(s)—make sure that at last one controller is switched on and connected to SteamVR—and press Play in the editor. When you press on the button with your hand (note: with your hand, not

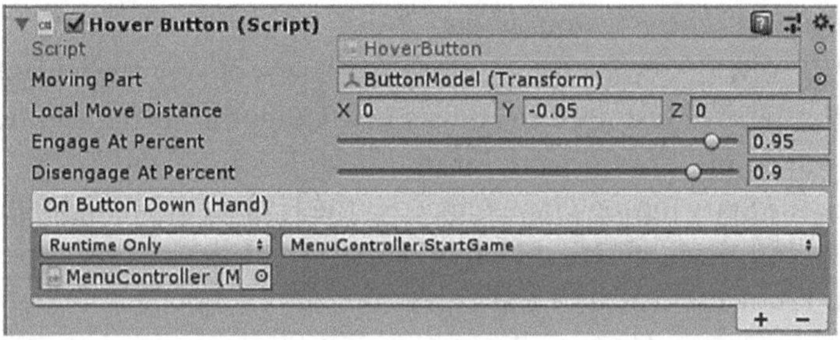

FIGURE 5.10 The Hover Button Component uses events to present a flexible way to call your own functions.

the controller itself) the button should move down and the main Scene should load.

This is a simple example of what you can do to make a physics-based, interactive main menu. When you make your own menus, use your imagination and try to build something that fits in with your VR universe. Experiment, have fun, and try to keep things interesting!

FADING IN AND OUT

You may have guessed it already—SteamVR takes care of fade ins and fade outs inside the headset. In this example, we will add a fade out effect to the exit game button so that our main menu will fade out nicely before it ends.

Add a Fade Out to the Main Menu

Open the example project for this chapter.

Open the main_menu Scene. Find the MenuController GameObject and click to show its properties in the Inspector. Double click on the script field in the Component, to open the script in the script editor.

Find the ExitGame() function:

```
public void ExitGame()
{
        Debug.Log("Exit game...");
}
```

After the Debug.Log statement, add the following line:

```
SteamVR_Fade.Start(Color.black, 2);
```

And you're done! Grab the headset and controllers, press Play in the editor, and when you select the Exit Game button your headset will fade nicely to black.

The SteamVR_Fade() function takes two parameters: a color and a fade time in seconds.

You can fade to any color using Unity's Color class—either using the presets like Color.black, Color.white, Color.blue, etc. or by using an RGB value like this:

```
new Color(1,1,1)
E.g. To fade out to white it would be:
SteamVR_Fade.Start(new Color(1,1,1), 2);
```

To fade in, if the screen is already faded out, you use Color.clear:

```
SteamVR_Fade.Start(Color.clear, 2);
```

To cut instantly to a color, without a fade effect, just use 0 for the time. For example:

```
SteamVR_Fade.Start(Color.blue, 0);
```

The completed MenuController.cs script should now look like this:

```
using UnityEngine;
using Valve.VR;

public class MenuController : MonoBehaviour
{
    public SteamVR_LoadLevel _levelLoader;

    public void StartGame()
    {
        Debug.Log("Start game...");

        // now tell SteamVR to load the main
game scene
        _levelLoader.levelName = "main_scene";
        _levelLoader.Trigger();
    }

    public void ExitGame()
    {
        Debug.Log("Exit game...");
        SteamVR_Fade.Start(Color.black, 2);
    }
}
```

MAKING YOUR OWN SKYBOX INSIDE UNITY

Earlier in this chapter, we looked at how to load Scenes correctly using SteamVR_LoadLevel to go the Compositor during loading. I mentioned that it is possible to use a custom skybox for the Compositor to display when SteamVR is loading.

Skyboxes are a traditional method used in videogame graphics to create the illusion of a sky around a 3D environment. The generated images are used to form a box that the Compositor renders around the view, creating the illusion of an environment in the same way a 360 video or panoramic photograph might work.

Using a skybox in VR is a good way to customize the Compositor to be more in keeping with your experience, but esthetically, the effect will not be an exact match of your Scene. Its scale will be different, and it may take a few attempts and some tweaking, but it can be worth doing to improve the overall flow of your experience.

To create your own skybox, you can use the SteamVR_Skybox Component. Think of this as a camera that you can put into the center of your Scene, and instead of snapping a picture in one direction, it will take multiple pictures for the front, back, left, right, top, and bottom images of a skybox.

Whenever you have the SteamVR_Skybox Component in your Scene, it will tell the Compositor to use this custom skybox whenever the Compositor takes over rendering to the headset.

Create a SteamVR Skybox for the Compositor

Open the example project for this chapter: Chapter 5—Project 2.

Open the main_menu Scene.

Create an empty GameObject (click the Create button at the top of the Hierarchy and choose Create Empty). Name the empty GameObject Skygen.

With the new Skygen GameObject selected, in the Inspector click the Add Component button. Choose Scripts > SteamVR_Skybox.

SteamVR_Skybox uses the current position and rotation of the GameObject that has the SteamVR Skybox Component on it (in this case, the Skygen GameObject). A good way to align it properly is to add a Camera Component to the same GameObject (Add Component > Camera) to see the viewpoint clearly.

Click the Take Snapshot button (Figure 5.11) to have Unity take a 360 view of the screen and build the skybox images for you. In the SteamVR Skybox Component, the image fields (Front, Back, Left, Right, Top, and Bottom) will be populated with some newly generated images.

Grab the headset and hit Play, to preview the Scene. You should be able to look around as normal, but if you go back to the Unity editor and hit the pause button, you will see the SteamVR Compositor takes control of rendering and displays your custom skybox.

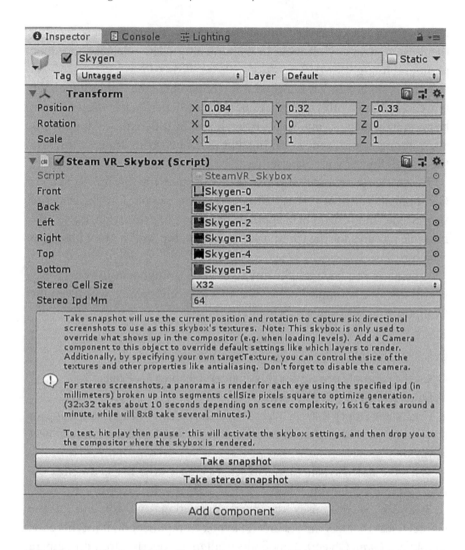

FIGURE 5.11 The SteamVR_Skybox Component will generate and apply textures for a skybox.

The images generated by the system are 2D captures from each direction around the camera (Figure 5.12). You can find all the images that this system generates in a folder automatically created with the same name as the Scene. In this case, a main_menu folder will appear in the Project browser.

You could reuse these images for other purposes, like effects for simulating reflection and so forth, if you wanted to.

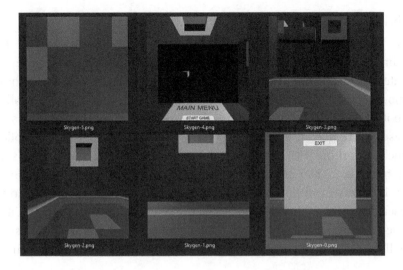

FIGURE 5.12   Images generated by the Steam VR_Skybox Component.

Using a Custom Skybox for Loading

Earlier in this chapter, we added a GameObject named LevelLoader with a SteamVR_Load Level Component attached to it, which can override the current Compositor's skybox and use a different one.

Highlight LevelLoader in the Hierarchy.

If you used the SteamVR_Skybox Component to generate your skybox, find the images in the Project browser (for example, the main_menu folder if you followed the example in the last section). SteamVR_Skybox does not name the images with front, back, left, right, top, or bottom in the names, but it does number them in the right order. That is,

0	Front
1	Back
2	Left
3	Right
4	Top
5	Bottom

Drag each image into the corresponding field of the SteamVR_Load Level Component, and it will then override Compositor settings to display this custom skybox during loading.

INTERACTION USING ONLY YOUR HEAD

As motion-tracked controllers were not yet commonplace in the first edition of this book, the UI system was based on where your gaze was. Interaction was handled by Unity's VR UI system, and it was all head-mounted. The main headsets now come equipped with tracked controllers, so it is assumed that you will use those for interaction; however, in some cases, there may be a time when you wish to do without the controllers, such as working with older hardware or building for accessibility. This section will demonstrate using a technique called raycasting to cast out an invisible ray from the headset and find out if there is a UI Button in the user's line of sight. When there is a Button found, the user can stare at it for a set amount of time (default is 3 seconds) to click it. A radial progress bar will show during the stare, to help users understand that the stare is timed.

Open the Example Project

Open the project Chapter 5—Project 3. Find the Scene named main_menu and open it in Unity.

In the Hierarchy, find and click on the GameObject named HeadInteractor. This GameObject contains everything we need for head-based interaction. Hold down the ALT key on the keyboard and click the little arrow next to its name, in the Hierarchy, to expand it out and show its child GameObjects. It looks like this:

HeadInteractor
      Cursor
           Canvas
                Image

The HeadInteractor GameObject has a Head Interactor Script Component attached to it. This is all the code to deal with (1) Finding out what the user is looking at and (2) Passing on hover start, hover end, and activate events to the UI buttons.

The cursor is a GameObject that is used to help show what the user is looking at. When we find out the exact hit point between the headset and button, this Cursor GameObject will be positioned there.

Canvas is a UI Canvas that contains a single child GameObject named Image. Image is a simple circular image that will be used as a progress display for the stare click system.

Click on the HeadInteractor, to show it in the Inspector.

On the Head Interactor Component, there are several fields. The most important one being Head for Raycast. This field needs a reference to the Camera that the headset is using. In the example Scene, the camera can be found under SteamVR's [CameraRig] prefab. If you use this script in your own project(s), be sure to populate this field for the script to work. The other fields—Cursor and Progress Image—are optional.

Right click on the Head Interactor Component and choose Edit Script, to open HeadInteractor.cs in the script editor.

The completed script looks like this:

```
// This script was adapted from Unity Interaction
Virtual Reality User Interface (VRUI) system's
VREyeRaycaster Component

using System;
using UnityEngine;

using Valve.VR.InteractionSystem;
using UnityEngine.UI;

public class HeadInteractor : MonoBehaviour
{
    public Transform headForRaycast;    // The start
point for the raycast / look detection

    [Space]
    public Transform cursor;        // A GameObject
to use as a cursor (with the progress UI attached
to it)
    public Image progressImage;    // An Unity UI
image set to Image Type Filled, to use as a stare
progress image

    [Space]
    public Vector3 rayPositionOffset;    // A
positional offset for the start of the raycast

    public LayerMask layerMask;    // Layers to
exclude from the raycast.
    private float rayLength = 500f;    // How far
into the scene the ray is cast.
```

```
        private GameObject currentInteractable;    //The
current interactive item
        private GameObject lastInteractable;       //The
last interactive item

        public float stareTimer;       // How long the
user has been staring at this item
        public float activateTime = 3;        // How long
you can stare until it counts as a click /
interaction

        [Space]
        public bool isEnabled;   // Should we even do
anything?

        private void Awake()
        {
            if (cursor != null)
            {
                // Hide the cursor
                cursor.gameObject.SetActive(false);
            }

            // Enable look detection
            isEnabled = true;
        }

        private void Update()
        {
            // Quick error check to make sure we have
a start point
            if (headForRaycast == null)
            {
                Debug.LogError("You need to set the
Transform to your Camera or FollowHead, on the Head
Pointer Component!");
                Debug.Break();
                return;
            }

            if (progressImage != null)
            {
                progressImage.fillAmount = 0;
```

```
                }

                // Call on the raycasting and detection
function if isEnabled is true...
                if (isEnabled)
                        EyeRaycast();
        }

        private void EyeRaycast()
        {
                // Work out the position from the
headForRaycast Transform with the rayPositionOffset
added to it
                Vector3 adjustedPosition = headForRaycast.
position + (headForRaycast.right *
rayPositionOffset.x) + (headForRaycast.up *
rayPositionOffset.y) + (headForRaycast.forward *
rayPositionOffset.z);

                // Create a ray that points forwards from
the camera.
                Ray ray = new Ray(adjustedPosition,
headForRaycast.forward);
                RaycastHit hit;

                // Do the raycast forwards to see if we
hit an interactive item
                if (Physics.Raycast(ray, out hit,
rayLength, layerMask))
                    {
                        if (cursor != null)
                        {
                            // Show the cursor, set its
position and rotation
                            cursor.gameObject.
SetActive(true);
                            cursor.position = hit.point;
                            cursor.rotation =
headForRaycast.rotation; //      The rotation matches
the head so that it should always be facing the camera
                        }

                        // See if the object we hit has a
Button Component attached to it
```

```
                Button aButton = hit.transform.
GetComponent<Button>();
                if (aButton == null)
                {
                        // No button was hit, so
deactivate the last interactive item.
                        DeactivateLastInteractable();
                        currentInteractable = null;
                        return;
                }

                // Grab the GameObject of the button
we hit
                currentInteractable = aButton.
gameObject;

                // If we hit an interactive item and
it's not the same as the last interactive item, then
call hover begin
                if (currentInteractable &&
currentInteractable != lastInteractable)
                {
                        // Use the SteamVR InputModule
to start a UI hover
                        InputModule.instance.HoverBegi
n(currentInteractable);
                }
                else if (currentInteractable ==
lastInteractable)
                {
                        // Count stare time and update
fillAmount of our progress display
                        stareTimer += Time.deltaTime;

                        if (progressImage != null)
                        {
                                progressImage.fillAmount
= (stareTimer / activateTime);
                        }

                        // If we have been staring for
longer than activateTime, count it as a click/
interaction
                        if (stareTimer > activateTime)
```

```
                    {
                            // Use the SteamVR
InputModule to tell the button we want to interact
with it
                            InputModule.instance.
Submit(currentInteractable);

                            // Reset the stare timer
                            stareTimer = 0;

                            // Clear out the
interactable store
                            DeactivateLastInteractable();

                            // Disable our look
detection for a bit after a click, then make a call to
ReEnable() to reenable it in x seconds
                            isEnabled = false;
                            Invoke("ReEnable", 1f);
                        }
                    }

                    // Deactivate the last interactive
item
                    if (currentInteractable !=
lastInteractable)
                            DeactivateLastInteractable();

                    lastInteractable =
currentInteractable;
                }
                else
                {
                    // Nothing was hit, deactive the
last interactive item.
                    DeactivateLastInteractable();
                    currentInteractable = null;
                }
        }

    void ReEnable()
    {
```

```
            // This is called after a click, to
reenable the button after a temporary switch off to
avoid accidental multiclicks
            isEnabled = true;
    }


    private void DeactivateLastInteractable()
    {
            // Reset stare timer and set the progress
image's fillAmount to zero
            stareTimer = 0;

            if (progressImage != null)
            {
                    progressImage.fillAmount = 0;
            }

            // If we don't have a reference to a
previously stored interactable object, drop out
            if (lastInteractable == null)
                    return;

            // Use SteamVR's InputModule to tell the
button that we're done with it (HoverEnd)
            InputModule.instance.HoverEnd
(lastInteractable);

            // Null the lastInteractable object store
            lastInteractable = null;

            if (cursor != null)
            {
                    // Hide the cursor
                    cursor.gameObject.SetActive(false);
            }
    }
}
```

Script Breakdown

The script was adapted from Unity's VRUI library VREyeRaycaster.cs
Component, which readers of the first edition of this book may recognize
as being the script used prior to this revision. SteamVR's UI Components
mean that, in this edition, Unity's VRUI is no longer used in this book.

Starting at the top:

```
using System;
using UnityEngine;

using Valve.VR.InteractionSystem;
using UnityEngine.UI;
```

The namespaces above are Unity standard ones for Unity scripts (System and UnityEngine) followed by the Valve.VR.InteractionSystem—giving us access to classes in the Interaction System that we need, like the InputModule used to tell UI elements to react. After that, we will need to know what a UI Button Component is further on in the script, and UnityEngine.UI will allow us to do that via access to UI classes like Button.

Following on, we are into the function declaration and variables. I have chosen to skip going through the variables line by line, as they should become clear as we move through the rest of the script. The Awake function follows on from there:

```
private void Awake()
{
        if (cursor != null)
        {
                // Hide the cursor
                cursor.gameObject.SetActive(false);
        }

        // Enable look detection
        isEnabled = true;
}
```

When the Scene loads, the cursor will be in whatever position it was set to during editing. This would look messy, so we start by hiding the cursor by setting its active property to false.

The variable isEnabled can disable or enable the core of this script. After loading, we want the look detection to be enable so that isEnabled is set to true here.

The Update() function is automatically called by Unity on all scripts, like this one, that derive from Monobehaviour (set in the class declaration):

```
private void Update()
{
```

```
            // Quick error check to make sure we have
a start point
            if (headForRaycast == null)
            {
                Debug.LogError("You need to set the
Transform to your Camera or FollowHead, on the Head
Pointer Component!");
                Debug.Break();
                return;
            }
```

Before diving in and running our main code, there is a quick check to make sure that a Camera has been referenced in the Inspector (or, at least, a similar Transform to denote where our head is). If headForRaycast variable is found to be null, we report an error to the Debug Log, call Debug.Break()—which stops playback in the editor—and drop out of the function to avoid any more code from being run.

After that, if isEnabled is true, a call to EyeRaycast() will do the actual look detection.

```
            // Call on the raycasting and detection
function if isEnabled is true...
            if (isEnabled)
                EyeRaycast();
        }
```

The EyeRaycast() is a fairly long function, we will split it up a bit to keep things clear:

```
        private void EyeRaycast()
        {
            // Work out the position from the
headForRaycast Transform with the rayPositionOffset
added to it
            Vector3 adjustedPosition = headForRaycast.
position + (headForRaycast.right *
rayPositionOffset.x) + (headForRaycast.up *
rayPositionOffset.y) + (headForRaycast.forward *
rayPositionOffset.z);
            // Create a ray that points forwards from
the camera.
```

```
        Ray ray = new Ray(adjustedPosition,
headForRaycast.forward);
        RaycastHit hit;
```

Raycasting can be imagined as a process involving drawing an invisible line from a start point in 3D space, out along a Vector (direction). If that line hits a GameObject with a Collider Component attached to it, Unity will tell us what the object is and where the hit occurred so that we can react to it. Perfect for this purpose!

When I first tested this, I found that the detection felt like it was a little low down. This could be down due to a few factors, such as the size of the colliders on the buttons. To compensate for that, I added a position adjustment. adjustedPosition is a variable that you can adjust in the Inspector on this Component to change where the ray will start from. I use the Transform's right, up, and forward vectors and multiply them by the corresponding adjustedPosition properties (x, y, or z) so that the position adjustment will use the rotation of the headForRaycast Transform. Our adjustment will be relative to the headForRaycast position.

A ray is created next (put into a variable of type Ray). Creating a Ray requires an origin/start position and direction, object using the adjustedPosition for its start position and headForRaycast.forward vector for its direction. The Ray, at this stage, has not yet been involved in any kind of detection. This will happen a little further down in the script. When we use Ray, it will return some information about its findings—such as a found object and hit point—that needs to be put into a variable of type RaycastHit. So, above, we declare a local scope variable named hit that will be used in the next line for the actual ray cast:

```
        // Do the raycast forweards to see if we
hit an interactive item
        if (Physics.Raycast(ray, out hit,
rayLength, layerMask))
        {
```

Physics.Raycast will carry out the ray cast and output its findings into that variable named hit. rayLength will determine how long the line will be. Remember that the Ray only says where to start and which direction to go in, and in the Physics.Raycast call we tell it how far to go.

To optimize the ray casting process, you can choose which collision layers will be included in the check. In this script, a variable named layerMask tells Physics.Raycast which layers we want to include. You can edit the included layers in Unity via a dropdown in the Inspector on this GameObject. For more information on collision layers, consult the Unity documentation.

At this stage, we have cast out a ray from the head into the 3D world. As it is in a conditional (if) statement, if the ray hits anything, it returns true and the code inside the brackets will run, which processes the ray hit:

```
if (cursor != null)
{
        // Show the cursor, set its
position and rotation
        cursor.gameObject.
SetActive(true);
        cursor.position = hit.point;
        cursor.rotation =
headForRaycast.rotation; //     The rotation matches
the head so that it should always be facing the camera
}
```

Now that we have found a Collider with a ray cast, the function can start to process it. If a cursor object has been set in the Inspector, this part of the code deals with positioning it to a place that will help the user.

The active property of the cursor's GameObject is set to true so that the cursor is visible. We set its position to the value held in that hit variable, which has the result from the ray cast in it. Finally, the cursor's rotation is set to the same rotation as our headForRaycast Transform. The intention here is that headForRaycast gives us a rotation to use so that the cursor will always be facing the camera. Matching the rotation of the cursor makes it easier for users to see. In this case, easier because the progress image is a child of the cursor, and the Canvas belonging to the progress image will move and rotate along with its parent Transform.

Before doing any specific UI-related action, the next chunk of code checks that we have hit a UI button and not some other GameObject on the same layer:

```
        // See if the object we hit has a
Button Component attached to it
```

```
                Button aButton = hit.transform.
GetComponent<Button>();
                if (aButton == null)
                {
                        // No button was hit, so
deactivate the last interactive item.
                        DeactivateLastInteractable();
                        currentInteractable = null;
                        return;
                }
```

Unity's GetComponent() function is used above to try to find a Button Component attached to the object detected by the ray cast. By trying to get to a Button like this, we can then do a null check to find out whether it was successful. If no Button Component was found, the variable aButton will be set to null by GetComponent(), and we can assume that this object is not a button. It is important to note that you MUST have a Collider attached to the same object that has the Button Component attached to it, for this to work.

Whenever aButton is null, we know that the object hit is not a button, and so we need to go ahead and reset things as though the ray had not hit anything.

This script needs to monitor the current object being looked at as well as the previous one. A little explanation of how this works:

1. An object is hit by the ray casting. We compare the hit object to the reference held in the variable lastInteractable to know whether this is a new object or if it is the one that we were already looking at.

2. If the object hit is new (and not already being looked at) we clear out lastInteractable variable and store a reference to the new object hit in a variable named currentInteractable.

3. At the end of processing the hit, lastInteractable is set to the value of currentInteractable so that we will know on the next cycle whether we are still looking at the same object or a new one.

DeactivateLastInteractable() will reset the variable lastInteractable. In the code above, we reset this when we do not detect a button from the ray cast. currentInteractable is also set to null and a return function drops out to ensure no more code is run on this pass.

The checks so far have made sure that the user is looking at a GameObject with a Collider attached, then checked that object is a button. Next up, the code will find out if this is a new GameObject or one we were already looking at:

```
// Grab the GameObject of the button we hit
                currentInteractable = aButton.
gameObject;
```

currentInteractable holds a reference to the GameObject being looked at. To get to this, we go via the aButton variable we set up earlier in this function. aButton contains a reference to the Button Component, but we can get to its GameObject with aButton.gameObject. In case you wonder why we are using GameObjects for currentInteractable and lastInteractable, we need a GameObject reference to pass into SteamVR further on.

```
                // If we hit an interactive item and
it's not the same as the last interactive item, then
call hover begin
                if (currentInteractable &&
currentInteractable != lastInteractable)
                {
                        // Use the SteamVR InputModule
to start a UI hover
                        InputModule.instance.HoverBegi
n(currentInteractable);
                }
```

As mentioned above, the code above checks that this is a new GameObject being looked at, by comparing currentInteractable to lastInteractable.

When we have something stored in currentInteractable and it is not the same object we were looking at previously (held in lastInteractable), the code above calls on InputModule—a SteamVR class—to give the button its behavior. InputModule.instance.HoverBegin() will force a rollover-type animation on to the button.

```
                else if (currentInteractable ==
lastInteractable)
                {
                        // Count stare time and update
fillAmount of our progress display
```

```
stareTimer += Time.deltaTime;
```

The code block above deals with what happens when we are "staring" at a button. That is, we look at the same object for more than one cycle of the script.

If currentInteractable and lastInteractable are the same, we add some time to a variable named stareTimer. This is used to keep track of how long the user has been looking at the button.

```
if (progressImage != null)
{
    progressImage.fillAmount
= (stareTimer / activateTime);
}
```

If we have an Image object in progressImage, above we set its.fillAmount property. When the Image Type is set to Filled (in the Inspector, on the actual image GameObject in the Scene), fillAmount will only display a portion of the image—an amount between 0 and 1 is used to say how much should be shown. Above, to calculate a value between 1 and 0 we take the current amount of time that the user has been staring (stareTimer) and divide it by the total time we allow them to stare at it before counting it as a click (activateTime).

Below, we deal with the click behavior:

```
                // If we have been staring for
longer than activateTime, count it as a click/
interaction
                if (stareTimer > activateTime)
                {
                    // Use the SteamVR
InputModule to tell the button we want to interact
with it
                    InputModule.instance.
Submit(currentInteractable);

                    // Reset the stare timer
                    stareTimer = 0;

                    // Clear out the
interactable store
DeactivateLastInteractable();
```

```
                    // Disable our look
detection for a bit after a click, then make a call to
ReEnable() to reenable it in x seconds
                    isEnabled = false;
                    Invoke("ReEnable", 1f);
        }
    }
```

If startTimer is greater than activateTime, the user has been looking at this button long enough for it to count as a click. InputModule is used, again to talk to the button via SteamVR, and we use its Submit() function to tell the button to act as though it has been clicked. The only parameter it needs to do that is the GameObject we are clicking—in the case above, a reference currentInteractable holds.

Now the interaction/click has happened, some resetting needs to be done to avoid any potential duplicate calls. The stareTimer is reset to 0, then a call to DeactivateLastInteractable() is made. Finally, isEnabled is set to false, so that this look detection will stop. Invoke calls a function after a given period of time. Above, Invoke is set to call the ReEnable function in 1 second, which should be enough time to avoid any duplicate interactions if the user continues to look at the button.

The last part of the EyeRaycast function:

```
                // Deactivate the last interactive
item
                if (currentInteractable !=
lastInteractable)
                        DeactivateLastInteractable();

                lastInteractable =
currentInteractable;
            }
```

The above code chunk is at the end of the "what happens when something is detected by the ray cast" condition. It deals with resetting lastInteractable, if needed, and setting it to the new GameObject ready for use in the next cycle.

If currentInteractable is not the same as lastInteractable, we reset lastInteractable with a call to DeactivateLastInteractable() just before setting lastInteractable to the current object being looked at (currentInteractable).

```
    else
    {
        // Nothing was hit, deactive the
last interactive item.
        DeactivateLastInteractable();
        currentInteractable = null;
    }
}
```

Finally in this function above, we deal with what happens when no object was found by the ray cast. DeactivateLastInteractable() resets the lastInteractable variable (and clears off any hover effect on the button, if needed) and we clear currentInteractable.

ReEnable is next in the class:

```
void ReEnable()
    {
        // This is called after a click, to
re-enable the button after a temporary switch off to
avoid accidental multiclicks
        isEnabled = true;
    }
```

isEnabled is set to true, above. ReEnable is called after the look detection is disabled after a click (by an Invoke statement further up). Once isEnabled is true, the Update() function will call EyeRaycast() again to do the detection.

```
private void DeactivateLastInteractable()
    {
        // Reset stare timer and set the progress
image's fillAmount to zero
        stareTimer = 0;

        if (progressImage != null)
        {
            progressImage.fillAmount = 0;
        }

        // If we don't have a reference to a
previously stored interactable object, drop out
```

```
        if (lastInteractable == null)
            return;

        // Use SteamVR's InputModule to tell the
button that we're done with it (HoverEnd)
        InputModule.instance.HoverEnd
(lastInteractable);

        // Null the lastInteractable object store
        lastInteractable = null;

        if (cursor != null)
        {
            // Hide the cursor
            cursor.gameObject.SetActive(false);
        }
    }
}
```

DeactivateLastInteractable() takes care of dealing with a reset, mostly being called when the viewer looks away from a button. It sets stareTimer to zero, sets the progressImage's fill amount to zero and, if lastInteractable is not null, will call on InputModule's HoverEnd() function to end the hover effect on the button we were previously looking at (held in lastInteractable). lastInteractable is set to null before we hide the cursor with cursor.gameObject.SetActive().

Back in Unity, with HeadInteractor selected in the Hierarchy, take a quick look at the Inspector to see the Head Interactor Component's properties. You should see a reference to the Camera in Head for Raycast, a Cursor in the Cursor field and a reference to the UI element named Image in the Progress Image field. Below that, the Ray position Offset and Layer Mask. The Layer Mask is set to UI. Always make sure that your own UI is on the same layer as set here in the HeadInteractor.

Finally on that Component, you can set the activate time to change how long you stare at something for it to count as a click.

RECAP

This chapter was about making a main menu, but we did so much more than that!

For a start, you learned how to make Unity GUI work with SteamVR tracked controllers. We looked at interacting with the UI using either the controllers themselves or by using a laser pointer system. As we built out the script to operate the laser pointer as a UI selector, you got to see how to detect an input action (our script reacted to the trigger press assigned to InteractUI). Knowing how to get to the controller actions will come in handy throughout this book. As if that was not enough, we also covered loading scenes correctly using the SteamVR_LoadLevel class, built a physics-based button, talked about using SteamVR_Fade to fade our Scenes in or out, and finished everything up with a quick section on making your own skybox using SteamVR_Skybox. After that, we looked at a completely different approach to UI that uses only the headset with a look detection script. Phew! That was a busy one!

In the next chapter, we will be gathering up all the skills learned so far to add functionality to a fun little game where you will have to protect yourself from giant insects! Let us spray!

CHAPTER 6

Advanced Interactions

I N THIS CHAPTER, WE ADD ADVANCED INTERACTION TO A GAME PROJECT. The game is a blaster where bugs fly at your head and you will need to spray them with bugspray to stop them stinging. SteamVR's Interaction system—specifically, the Interactable and Modal Throwable Components—is used to make spray bottles that can be picked up and sprayed at the bugs. As well as making a working spray bottle, this chapter will add a custom pose to the SteamVR hand, so that the hand holds and sprays the bottle in a realistic way.

To complement the SteamVR Components, we build a custom script, SprayController.cs, revisiting the method of getting input from the controllers used earlier in this book, from Chapter 5: Add Controller Input to the Laser Pointer.

OPEN THE EXAMPLE PROJECT

Open the example project for this chapter in the Chapter 6 folder.

Find and open the main_scene Scene in the Project Browser.

Adding Spray Functionality to the Spray Bottle

In the previous chapter, we looked at detecting an action from the controllers and reacting to it to activate a button with the laser pointer. Using the same principles here, in this section we look at getting the input from our controllers that make the spray bottles work.

The great thing about the script we will look at in this section is that it can be repurposed for many other uses. It detects an action and uses an event to call a function. The function can be on any GameObject, in any script, which makes it flexible.

Find the Prefabs folder in the Project browser. Inside that folder, look for the SprayPrefab object and click on it to see its Components in the Inspector. Find the SprayController Component in the Inspector and right click on it. Choose Edit Script to open the script in the script editor.

```
using System.Collections;
using System.Collections.Generic;
using UnityEngine;
using UnityEngine.Events;

using Valve.VR;
using Valve.VR.InteractionSystem;

public class ControllerInput : MonoBehaviour
{
        public SteamVR_Action_Boolean interactAction =
SteamVR_Input.GetAction<SteamVR_Action_
Boolean>("default", "Trigger_Press");
        public SteamVR_Action_Vibration hapticAction =
SteamVR_Input.GetVibrationAction("default", "haptic",
false);

        [Space]
        public bool do_haptic_buzz = true;
        public float haptic_duration = 0.1f;
        public float haptic_freq = 250f;
        public float haptic_amplitude = 0.1f;

        [Space]
        public UnityEvent OnActionEvent;
        public UnityEvent OnActionEndEvent;

        private SteamVR_Input_Sources myHand;
        private Interactable _interactableComponent;

        private bool isON;

        void Start()
    {
            // grab a ref to the Interactable
Component
            _interactableComponent = GetComponent
<Interactable>();
```

```
        }

    void Update()
    {
            // make sure we're being held before
trying to find out what's holding us
            if (_interactableComponent.attachedToHand
== null)
                return;

            // get the hand currently holding this
spray bottle
            myHand = _interactableComponent.attached
ToHand.handType;

            // double check that the hand value
returned is valid
            if (myHand == null)
                return;

            // if the state has just started (down)
then we spray..
            if (interactAction[myHand].stateDown)
            {
                if (!isON)
                {
                    ActionStart();
                    isON = true;
                }
            } else
            {
                if(isON)
                {
                    isON = false;
                    ActionEnd();
                }
            }
    }

    void ActionStart()
    {
            // take care of the haptics
            if(do_haptic_buzz)
```

```
                   hapticAction.Execute(0, haptic_
duration, haptic_freq, haptic_amplitude, myHand);

          // fire off the unity event
          OnActionEvent.Invoke();
     }

     void ActionEnd()
     {
          OnActionEndEvent.Invoke();
     }
 }
```

Script Breakdown

At the top of the script are the using package declarations:

```
using System.Collections;
using System.Collections.Generic;
using UnityEngine;
using UnityEngine.Events;

using Valve.VR;
using Valve.VR.InteractionSystem;
```

As well as the standard UnityEngine, System.Collections and System.Collections.Generic, for talking to SteamVR, we need Valve.VR and, for the Interaction system specifically, Valve.VR.InteractionSystem.

The class derives from Monobehaviour, so there is nothing special to note about that. After the class declaration we set up some variables:

```
public class SprayController : MonoBehaviour
{
     public SteamVR_Action_Boolean interactAction =
SteamVR_Input.GetAction<SteamVR_Action_
Boolean>("default", "Trigger_Press");
     public SteamVR_Action_Vibration hapticAction =
SteamVR_Input.GetVibrationAction("default", "haptic",
false);
```

Above, the first two variables are perhaps the most interesting because we declare them and attempt to populate them at the same time. The variable interactAction is of type SteamVR_Action—linked directly to the Actions system from the SteamVR Input window, we looked at in previous chapters (e.g. Unity from Chapter 3—Setting Up SteamVR Input), which in turn is linked to the Steam Bindings system we covered in Chapter 5. Essentially, a SteamVR_Action is an input event. In the variable above, the event we look for is called "Trigger_Press," and it can be found under the "default" set of actions in the bindings system. To see all the actions in the project, go to Window>SteamVR Input. The SteamVR Input window shows all the available action sets and actions within them that you can use here in code, in this manner. You can also add your own action sets or actions as required.

After we set up the action we want to look for in interactAction, the next line declares a variable named hapticAction of the type SteamVR_Action_Vibration. Again, returning to SteamVR_Actions we can see that the default action set contains an action named "haptic." Unlike other SteamVR actions, we use this one to output a little vibration buzz via the controller when users squeeze the trigger. A little haptic feedback can help realism, even when it is not an exact replica of the feedback you might get in the real world—having some form of feedback will always be better than none. It serves to reinforce the interaction as a physical action rather than just a simulated image. In virtual reality, giving everything rules, making everything as interactive as possible and providing logical feedback for user action is key to an immersive experience. If you are ever unsure about an action because it feels kind of hollow, add a little buzz of haptic feedback like this and see if it helps!

The next variables are the parameters used for the haptic feedback:

```
[Space]
public bool do_haptic_buzz = true;
public float haptic_duration = 0.1f;
public float haptic_freq = 250f;
public float haptic_amplitude = 0.1f;
```

From the top, there is "do_haptic_buzz" which can be set on or off inside the Inspector, which will turn on or off the haptic buzz. Although it is not needed in the example project, I understand that you might not always want the haptic buzz with every interaction if you use this script in your own projects, so I have included this to make the script that little bit more flexible.

The variables haptic_duration, haptic_freq, and haptic_amplitude control the duration, frequency, and amplitude of the buzz. These parameters directly affect how the actual haptic feedback will be generated by the controller and how it will feel to the user. Do feel free to play around with these numbers to see what they do and how they affect the feeling of pressing the trigger. To change them, open the SprayBottle prefab from inside the Prefabs folder in the Project explorer, then alter them via the Inspector (Figure 6.1).

The next five variable declarations look like this:

```
[Space]
public UnityEvent OnActionEvent;
public UnityEvent OnActionEndEvent;

private SteamVR_Input_Sources myHand;
private Interactable _interactableComponent;

private bool isON;
```

OnActionEvent and OnActionEndEvent were declared as UnityEvents. A UnityEvent shows up in the Inspector in a way that allows you to point at any GameObject in the Scene. You can then choose a public function from a script Component attached to that GameObject, and whenever this event gets fired by your script, it will call that specified remote function. Being able to choose what gets called when our actions are activated like this makes

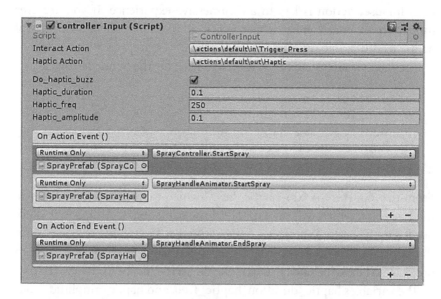

FIGURE 6.1 The SprayBottle has a ControllerInput Component. Its values in the Inspector may be changed to alter the feel of its haptic feedback vibrations.

the script flexible and capable of being reused in a wide range of scenarios. For example, you could have a light fitting attached to a wall that has the Interactable Component attached to it. After attaching this script to the light fitting, you could trap a trigger press that calls on a function on another GameObject to turn the light on or off. Another obvious example might be a weapon—you could detect the trigger the same as we do for the spray bottle, only you would have those OnActionEvent and OnActionEndEvent call out to another script to fire out a projectile or laser blast.

The myHand variable of type SteamVR_Input_Sources is key to controller communication. The variable myHand will be used in the main loop to tell which hand is holding this GameObject. For more information on the SteamVR_Input_Sources type, refer back to Chapter 5—"Add Controller Input to the Laser Pointer" in the "Script Breakdown" section.

This script will be populating the myHand variable a little differently to how we did back in Chapter 5. In this class, we use a nifty method of finding out which hand is interacting with our GameObject via the Interactable Component. A reference to the attached Interactable Component is stored in _interactableComponent and we set this up automatically (always assuming that the Interactable Component is attached to the same GameObject) with GetComponent() next, in the Start() function.

As Start() is automatically called by the game engine when the Scene starts, it is the perfect place to grab any object or Component references we might need later in the script:

```
void Start()
{
        // grab a ref to the Interactable
Component
        _interactableComponent = GetComponent
<Interactable>();
}
```

As we can now access the Interactable Component via _interactable-Component, the Update() function can start out by checking to see if any interaction is happening:

```
void Update()
{
        // make sure we're being held before
trying to find out what's holding us
```

```
            if (_interactableComponent.attachedToHand
== null)
                  return;
```

In the frame update's Update() function, it is important to check that the Interactable Component has a valid reference to a hand before trying to find out which hand it might be. A simple null check takes care of that, above, and as long as _interactableComponent.attachedToHand does not null, we can go ahead and access that to get to the its.handType property to find out which hand is holding the spray bottle. handType is a SteamVR_Input_Sources type enumerator that provides a description of the hand, not the actual Hand object itself:

```
            // get the hand currently holding this
spray bottle
            myHand = _interactableComponent.
attachedToHand.handType;
            // double check that the hand value
returned is valid
            if (myHand == null)
                  return;
```

Once we have the hand type in the variable handType, interactAction is used to find its state:

```
            // if the state has just started (down)
then we spray..
            if (interactAction[myHand].state)
            {
                  if (!isON)
                  {
                        ActionStart();
                        isON = true;
                  }
            } else
            {
                  if(isON)
                  {
                        isON = false;
                        ActionEnd();
                  }
            }
      }
```

interactAction will return either true or false. It is an object used to get access to the state of actions. What happens above is that we ask about the state of the action (the action specified by interactAction) on the hand described by myHand. If this action's state is true, we know that the user is trying to interact with the spray bottle and we can make the call to the function ActionStart() or otherwise, if this returns false, call to ActionEnd(). To help keep tabs on the current state, isON is also set to true or false depending on the action state returned from interactAction.

The ActionStart() function is next:

```
void ActionStart()
{
        // take care of the haptics
        if(do_haptic_buzz)
                hapticAction.Execute(0, haptic_
duration, haptic_freq, haptic_amplitude, myHand);

        // fire off the unity event
        OnActionEvent.Invoke();
}
```

We will look at the haptics in detail further on, in the "Haptics" section of this chapter. In this class, do_haptic_buzz is a bool provided for your convenience. You can turn on or off the haptic effect by checking the do_haptic_buzz checkbox in the Inspector, which will depend on whatever you are using this script for. In the case of the spray bottle, we want the haptic buzz to be set to on.

After the call to make the controller buzz, a call is made to the OnActionEvent.Invoke() function. What this does is to fire the OnActionEvent UnityEvent we discussed in the variable declarations. On the spray bottle, the UnityEvents in the Inspector are set up to both create the spray and to animate the handle (Figure 6.2).

The last part of this script is the ActionEnd() function:

```
void ActionEnd()
{
        OnActionEndEvent.Invoke();
}
```

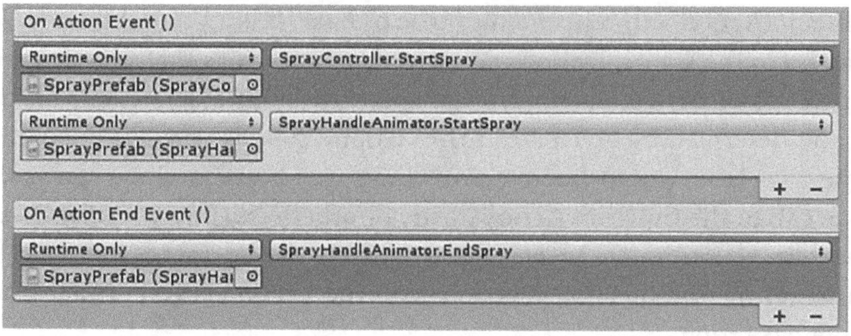

FIGURE 6.2 UnityEvents are set up in the Inspector on the Controller Input Component to communicate with the Spray Controller and Spray Animation Controller scripts.

OnActionEndEvent is another UnityEvent. In the Inspector (Figure 6.6), it is set to tell the spray bottle's animation script that the spray has finished. The animation script can then animate the handle back to its idle position.

USING VIBRATION/HAPTIC FEEDBACK

As seen in the script from the previous section, SteamVR provides a method for haptic feedback through its SteamVR_Action_Vibration class. In this section, I wanted to provide a little bit of information, separate from the example project, on how you can implement this for yourself in your own scripts.

To use haptics, you start with a variable declaration like this:

```
public SteamVR_Action_Vibration hapticAction =
SteamVR_Input.GetVibrationAction("default", "haptic",
false);
```

You will also need a hand type to tell the hapticAction which hand to vibrate on. In the script from the previous section, we found the hand by looking at the Interactable Component's attachedHand variable. In Chapter 5, however, when we added controller input to the laser pointer, the hand was set in the Unity Inspector instead. To declare the hand so that it can be set in the Inspector you can make a public SteamVR_Input_Sources type variable like this:

```
public SteamVR_Input_Sources myHand;
```

Then, any time you want to make a controller vibrate, the syntax is

```
hapticAction.Execute(seconds_from_now, haptic_
duration, haptic_frequency, haptic_amplitude, myHand);
```

SETTING UP THE SKELETON POSER TO USE A HAND POSE

The first step to adding hand poses to an object is to add the Steam VR_ Skeleton_Poser script Component to the Interactable object you want to use a hand pose with.

In the Project browser, find the Prefabs folder and, inside that, the SprayPrefab GameObject. Click SprayPrefab to highlight it and, over in the Inspector, click the Open Prefab button. This will open the Prefab as though it has an entire Scene all to itself. Don't panic! The main Scene is safe. Unity opens prefabs to edit like this and will restore the previous Scene once you Save or close the Prefab.

The SprayPrefab GameObject should be highlighted already. If not, click on it in the Hierarchy to highlight it.

In the Inspector, click Add Component. In the search box, start typing Skeleton_Poser until the Steam VR_Skeleton_Poser Component appears in the menu. Add Steam VR_Skeleton_Poser to the SprayPrefab GameObject.

The Skeleton Poser Component

There are two tabs in the Skeleton Poser Component (Figure 6.3). One is the Pose Editor, which is used for creating and editing poses, and the other deals with blending poses together.

The Pose Editor

At this point of the chapter, you can choose to create a pose from scratch or use an existing pose I have made for you and included in the example project files. Poses are saved in Unity as ScriptableObjects that you can easily reuse across different objects and projects.

If you do choose to use a premade pose, you should still read through the upcoming "How the Spray Bottle Got Its Hierarchy" section later in this chapter, for some useful information on making your own poses in the future.

Use the Premade Pose To load the premade example pose, find the Assets/Pose_premade folder in the Project browser. In that folder is a pose

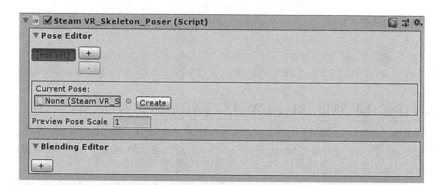

FIGURE 6.3 The SteamVR_Skeleton_Poser Component.

file named CanGrab. Drag it out of the Project browser and drop it into the Current Pose text field on the Steam VR_Skeleton_Poser Component.

Create Your Own Pose To create your own pose, click the Create button to the right of the Current Pose field in the Inspector (Figure 6.4). Unity will ask where to save the new file. In the file browser, choose the Poses folder and name the pose CanGrab. For now, follow the instructions in this chapter. You will get to create the pose in the next section of this chapter, "Posing Your Hand."

With a pose in the Current Pose field, the Skeleton Poser Component should now open to show more configuration options (Figure 6.5) and, under Current Pose, you should see the CanGrab pose in the field.

The left and right images of hands are clickable. Click them to toggle on or off a hand preview in the Scene window. You will most likely build your

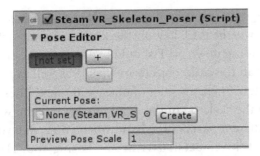

FIGURE 6.4 You can create your own poses by clicking on the Create button in the Steam VR_Skeleton Poser Component.

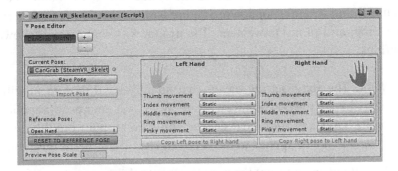

FIGURE 6.5 The SteamVR_Skeleton_Poser Component with a new pose and preview toggle hand buttons.

basic pose with just one hand enabled in the preview and then enable them both at the same time so that the copy buttons become available and you can copy over the pose from one hand to the other.

For now, make sure that the right hand preview is enabled and that the left hand preview is disabled.

In the Hierarchy, the SprayPrefab layout should look something like this:

```
SprayPrefab
        SprayBottleParent
                SprayBottle
                        HandleParent
                                Handle
                        SprayPoint
        vr_glove_right_model_slim(Clone)
        UICanvas
                AmmoNum
```

The vr_glove_right_model_slim GameObject also has an arrow next to it. Hold down the ALT key on the keyboard and click the arrow to expand it. Holding down ALT should expand out the child objects too, meaning that all the child objects are visible as well as any of their own child objects too. There are a lot of objects in there! These are the bones that make up the skeleton of the hand model, and you will use these to choose the different parts of the hand when you create your own poses. We will look at this in detail later in the "Posing Your Hand" section in this chapter.

The Steam VR_Skeleton_Poser Component offers several options for how the animations are applied to the hands. Below the hand images, you can find several dropdowns (Figure 6.6) for the thumb, index, middle, ring, and pinky movement. The dropdowns contain the following options:

Static: The Static setting means that no additional movement will be applied to the pose that you create. Whenever your pose is applied to the hand, any additional skeletal animation input from the controller will not be applied to the hand, and it will stay in the pose you set.

Free: If you do not want the pose to apply to this finger, choose free and SteamVR will apply only the skeletal pose from controller tracking. This is useful when you want to pose only certain fingers, but you would like users to retain control over the others via the tracking on the controllers.

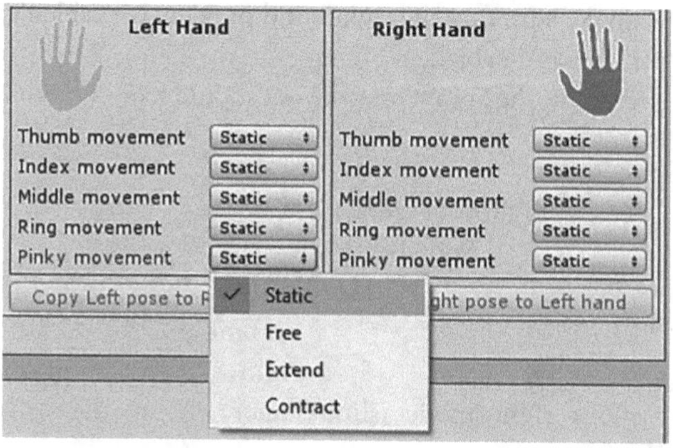

FIGURE 6.6 The SteamVR Skeleton_Poser Additive Dropdown Menus.

Extend: With this mode, the pose you apply will be the minimum grip applied to the hand, and anything coming in from the controllers will be added to it.

Contract: This works like Extend, except the opposite. The pose you apply will act as the maximum grip, with controller skeletal input added to contract the grip.

At the very bottom of the SteamVR Skeleton_Poser Component is the Preview Pose Scale field. This is used when you are applying scaling to the VR camera and you need to scale the poses up or down. For now and for normal use, you can leave this at 1.

The Blending Editor

The Blending Editor provides a method for blending between poses so that they appear to transition smoothly in the application. We will look at the Blending Editor further in this chapter, in the "Blending Poses" section.

Posing Your Hand

Now that you have all the bones visible in the Hierarchy, we can start to manipulate them to wrap around the spray bottle.

When setting up your pose, the main thing to remember is not to rotate or move the hand itself—move the object to the hand and pose the hand in place. You can manipulate the bones within the hand, but moving or rotating the entire hand will have no effect on the final animation. Even changes to the Root bone or the wrist_r bone will have no effect.

To achieve the position and rotation to make this work, you may need to do some additional work in the Hierarchy, such as adding empty GameObjects to use as parent objects. With the SprayPrefab Prefab, I have already done the necessary parenting of objects and, in the next section, we look at how this came about and why the objects are structured inside the Prefab the way they are.

How the Spray Bottle Got Its Hierarchical Structure To illustrate some of the problems a GameObject structure can present when making your hand poses, this section will show you how the SprayPrefab GameObject in the example project got to its current hierarchical structure.

The most obvious approach to creating objects is to take a 3D model, drag it into the Scene, and turn it into a GameObject. For example, the spray bottle started out like this in the Hierarchy:

SprayBottleModel   This can cause an issue if you need to scale or rotate the model, since anything else you want to add to it (any child objects or Components) will then become affected by the scale. This is also a problem for SteamVR_Skeleton_Poser as we do not want the hand to be locked to the scale and rotation of the bottle model. The two need to be independent of each other, in terms of scale and rotation.

It is better to start with an empty GameObject and make the 3D model a child of the empty GameObject. I named the empty GameObject Spray_BottleParent. So, the next step in the evolution of the spray bottle Prefab looked like this:

> SprayBottleParent
> SprayBottle

Now, we are free to rotate the spray can model as required, but I had trouble with manipulating scale and rotation of my spray bottle GameObject directly. To avoid problems, another empty GameObject is called for! This time, I created an empty GameObject and named it SprayPrefab and added everything so far to it, to be child objects. At this stage, the structure looked like this:

> SprayPrefab
> SprayBottleParent
> SprayBottle

With the model and hierarchy all set up, I added Steam VR_Skeleton_Poser to the SprayPrefab GameObject and clicked on the hand preview so that SteamVR would automatically add the hand model into the Scene. With the hand enabled, my structure looks like:

> SprayPrefab
> SprayBottleParent
> SprayBottle
> vr_glove_right_model_slim(Clone)

As you can see above, the hand is on the same level as the SprayBottleParent—a child of the SprayPrefab GameObject. In this format, we can manipulate scale and rotation of SprayBottleParent without affecting the hand.

In Figure 6.7, you can see how the hand pose was constructed. From left to right:

1. Both position and rotation do not match the hand. It seems to be pointing down from the top left to the top of the can.

2. Rather than rotating the hand (which does not work), the entire SprayPrefab GameObject is rotated so that the hand is straight—at the same sort of angle we need for the final pose.

3. Next up, the SprayBottleParent GameObject was rotated into place so that it sits in the palm of the hand and we can bend the figures around it, to grab it.

4. The finished hand pose and can rotation. Note that the bottle is a physics object, which has a Mesh Collider attached to SprayBottle (the 3D model GameObject). Since the Collider is attached to the SprayBottle object, its collider will remain correct regardless of how we rotate or move the SprayBottleParent GameObject or the bottle object.

The main thing to remember when posing the hand is not to rotate or move the hand itself—move the object to the hand and pose the hand in place.

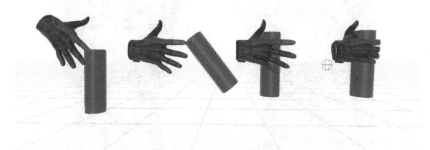

FIGURE 6.7   The evolution of the spray bottle rig.

Creating Your Own Pose   All that is left to do is for you to make your own pose. This is where your creative side will come in handy. You need to use the rotate tools to rotate the bones of the hand until the pose looks something like holding a spray bottle (Figure 6.8).

Try to pay attention to how the texture stretches when you rotate the bones and try not to make any stretching look too obvious. It may take some playing around with, to get right. If you have trouble, I have provided a completed pose in the example project named CanGrab_Complete and you can find that in the Pose_premade folder. Just drag that into the Current Pose field to skip having to pose this yourself.

With your pose completed, click the SprayPrefab GameObject in the Hierarchy again to show the Steam VR_Skeleton Poser Component.

Click the right-hand image so that the right-hand preview appears in the Scene view.

Below the right-hand panel in that Skeleton Poser Component, find and click the Copy Right Pose to Left Hand button. Click Confirm when the confirmation window asks if you want to overwrite the current left-hand pose.

FIGURE 6.8   The completed skeleton pose for holding a spray can.

Your pose will be automatically copied over to the left hand (Figure 6.9). Click the Save Pose button to save your pose.

At this stage, I should mention that it is a good idea to back up your work regularly. When working on complex poses, you may want to clone the ScriptableObject pose file at various stages along the way just to make sure that you can revert to previous versions if needed.

Blending Poses

Having a completed pose ready to go, the next step is to tell SteamVR how to blend the hand animation to your pose.

In the Blending Editor panel—in the Inspector when your GameObject containing Steam VR_Skeleton_Poser is selected—click the + button to add a blend.

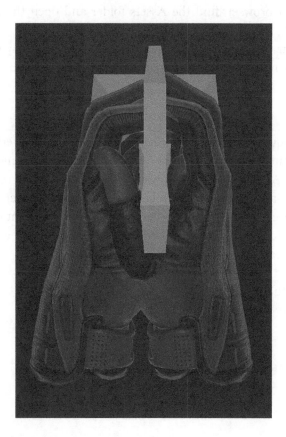

FIGURE 6.9 The skeleton pose is automatically copied over to the left hand when you click the copy button.

Starting from the top, you can give the blend a name by typing into the Name field. Type blend in there now, to name the blend.

Below the Name field is a slider for Influence. This affects how much your skeletal pose will affect the regular pose of the hand. If you only wanted to affect the hand in a small way, you would slide this down to a lower value. As we want the full effect of your pose to be applied to the hand in this example; leave it at 1.

TRY OUT THE SCENE

In the Inspector, click the Left Hand and Right Hand graphics to turn off the hand previews. Click the Save button at the top of the Scene pane, to save the Prefab. To the left of the SprayPrefab GameObject, in the Hierarchy, click on the small left-pointing arrow (just below the Create button) to return to the main Scene and close the Prefab editor.

In Project browser, find the Assets folder and open the main_menu Scene.

Grab your tracked controllers and headset and press Play in the editor to play. When you pick up a spray bottle, it should use your new pose to wrap!

RECAP

We packed quite a lot of useful techniques into this chapter! We looked at the example project and how the spray bottle is connected to the controllers. After that, haptic feedback provided a solid reinforcement of the spray action before we looked at the Skeleton Poser system. The Skeleton Poser can be used to pose hands around different objects for a more realistic simulation, so we ended this chapter with a quick crash course on creating your own poses.

In the next chapter, we will look at Unity's audio system and how to set it up for virtual reality.

CHAPTER 7

Making the Most of Virtual Reality with Audio

THE VIRTUAL REALITY AUDIO SPACE AND BEYOND

A headset can only go so far in replacing the viewer's senses. To make the virtual seem real, we must envelop our users in our universes. Visual and audio senses should complement each other, working together to create a rounded experience. If visual and audio do not work together, the illusion of the virtual world will fall short.

Sound engineering and sound design is a deep and wide-ranging subject that could easily merit its own book (such as *The Game Audio Tutorial: A Practical Guide to Sound and Music for Interactive Games*, by Richard Stevens and Dave Raybould, published by CRC Press in 2011). It may seem obvious, but I need to iterate that what I could squeeze into a chapter is not going to qualify you to be a sound engineer. The process of audio design is all too often overlooked. Particularly so in games and simulation design, many studios leave audio until the end of a production or skimping on the audio budget. It is a common mistake and one that can ruin an otherwise amazing experience. Audio can make or break it. As well as reinforcing the themes of the experience, audio can guide the player, subtle accents can influence emotion, and music can set a pace and give a game a heartbeat. If you find a good sound engineer to work with you should be extremely nice to them and make sure you give them plenty of time to do their job and not have to rush!

Software

In this chapter, we only use one third-party audio system—Steam virtual reality (SteamVR)—and it is free to use both commercially and noncommercially. You do not need to use Steam Audio and you can easily get by with Unity's built-in sound system and an audio editor program. For download instructions, see the "Using Steam Audio for VR" section later in this chapter.

For audio editing and recording, I recommend Audacity, an opensource, cross-platform audio editor and recorder. I will not be covering it in this book, but Audacity is useful for recording audio as well as doing things like normalizing the volumes (to keep the audio levels around the same levels), cutting audio for loops, and many other common audio tasks. Download Audacity for free, from audacityteam.org.

Common Terms

To be able to discuss the techniques in this chapter, it is necessary to clarify some terms that you may or may not have heard elsewhere. Some terms are specific to games and simulation development, some specific to Unity and some common terms used in audio engineering.

Ambient Sound

Ambient sound is a type of audio that plays in the background, reinforcing the main themes of the scene. This could be something as simple as birds chirping to fill an outdoor scene or a low rumble inside a spaceship. Ambient audio can be simple or complex, sometimes dynamically created and consisting of multiple layers of real or synthetic sounds.

Listener

In Unity, a listener is a Component that acts as the ears of a scene. Whatever the listener would "hear" from wherever the Listener Component is positioned is what will be played out through the sound hardware of the computer. The standard listener gives a good enough experience, but it is not accurate to how a person would normally hear. You could imagine the standard Unity listener as a single ear pointing forward from wherever it stands in the 3D space. Sound will appear to be coming from a circular radius around its position. A human head, on the other hand, would often have two ears pointing out from each side of the head, making the positional tracking more accurate and easier for a human to distinguish spatial differences.

Binaural Audio

Binaural audio is the method of recording audio with two microphones positioned in such a way as to represent two ears. Some binaural microphones go so far as to be shaped like ears to give a visual representation of how the listener will be spatially positioned in the audio world. When the sound engineer records the sounds, they can see exactly where the listener is and adjust the positions of objects to be recorded to get the desired effect. This system is relatively new to videogames, and it is still rare for game studios to employ these types of recording methods due to the high price of quality binaural recording equipment as well as the extra time and effort required to master it correctly.

Mono Sound

Unity refers to single channel audio as mono sound. In this context, the word mono is used as an abbreviation for the term monophonic, which means a sound coming from a single channel of transmission. A mono sound will normally sound as if it is coming directly from in front of the listener when it is played outside of a 3D scene. When you use a mono sound in the 3D world, its attributes like its sound volume, panning, and effects are adjusted based on where it is in the world. You can use mono sounds for objects that emit sound in the 3D world, such as machinery or doors and so on, so that approaching the object will influence how it sounds.

3D Sound

Despite the name, 3D sound in Unity is not linked spatially to the camera, viewer, or listener. It is a sound that is already mastered to have its own 3D space encoded in the audio file. If you try to play a 3D sound at a specific point in space, without changing its audio emitter settings, the only thing that will be affected by its spatial positioning will be the volume that it plays at.

Doppler Effect

If you have ever heard an emergency vehicle go by with its sirens blazing, you may have noticed the way that the pitch of the sound changes depending on how near or far away from you it is. This is known as the Doppler effect, which is caused by the way sound waves travel. Unity's sound system will attempt to duplicate this effect for a more realistic movement in the audio space.

Spatial Sound

Spatial sound refers to audio that sounds as though it exists in a three-dimensional space; sound can flow all around the listener so that audio emitters sound like it comes from its virtual position.

HRTF

Head-Related Transfer Function (HRTF) is basically the way that our head interprets sound. The way we interpret audio is affected by what the sound hits on its way to the eardrum. Amazingly, our brains can sense subtle changes in the audio—acoustic alterations—that help it to understand which direction the sounds are coming from. When we talk about HRTF and VR, we are usually talking about simulating changes in audio frequencies to reproduce the effects of HRTF and fool the brain's spatial interpretation.

Steam Audio

Valve offers its own audio system for environment and listener simulation. Although it is ideal for VR audio, it is not exclusive to VR and could be used for any type of application. Valve offers Steam Audio free of charge, and it can be used either out of the box or in conjunction with FMOD.

FMOD

FMOD is a premium audio solution intended for game development. It features a wide-ranging toolset for mastering and engineering audio, including an editor and API. We will not cover FMOD in this book.

USING UNITY AUDIO FOR VR

Open the Example Project

Open the Unity project for this chapter from the folder Chapter 7—Project 1—Unity Audio.

Grab your headset, press Play in the editor and give it a try. The example project for this chapter is almost the same as the previous chapter. In this project, the audio has been removed and there are no ground-based bugs. In this section, we go through the steps to add audio to the project as a practical exercise on how to set up audio for VR.

Unity Audio Settings

Open the Project Settings window (Edit > Project Settings) and choose Audio from the list on the left of the window (Figure 7.1).

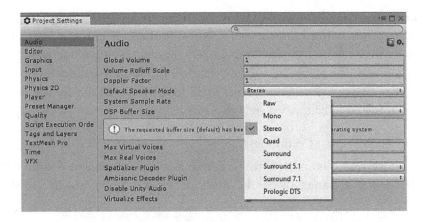

FIGURE 7.1   The Audio settings panel in Project Settings.

By default, Unity audio is set to be mastered in Stereo. This means 2-channel audio (left and right speakers) and not surround sound. If your headset, headphones or sound system supports surround sound your project will not be utilizing the whole audio space. Correct this by choosing Surround from the Default Speaker Mode dropdown in the Audio settings menu.

Surround sets the channel count to a 5.5 speaker setup. This includes front left, front right, center, rear left, and rear right. You can specify more complicated setups such as 5.1, 7.1, or ProLogic systems if required. As a side note, if you wanted to give users a configurable option, add a settings menu to your project using the AudioSettings.Reset class to change the device configuration through code.

Just a note on this; the standard Unity audio system is very good at delivering high-quality surround sound audio, but if you want to generate more realistic acoustics you should look to a third-party solution such as Steam Audio. We will look at Steam Audio, briefly, further in this chapter in "Using Steam Audio for VR."

Setting a Scene with Ambient Sound

Imagine audio as a series of layers. Often, you are hearing many different layers playing at the same time. As you walk down a city street, for example, you could be hearing cars, birds singing, people talking, distant horns beeping, and an airplane passing by. You may have walked along the street a hundred times before and your focus may be on a conversation you are having with someone else along the way, but those ambient layers of sound help your brain to know and understand the environment you are in. Many of them need to be heard. There are layers of sound that you might never notice until they stopped being there. If just a few of those layers were missing, you will most likely register that there is something wrong with the scene. In a VR experience, the sounds around us have a similar effect in giving our brains extra information about the world we are supposed to believe we are a part of.

The AudioSource Component

In Unity, sound is emitted from an AudioSource Component (Figure 7.2) attached to a GameObject. The Audio Listener, usually attached to the

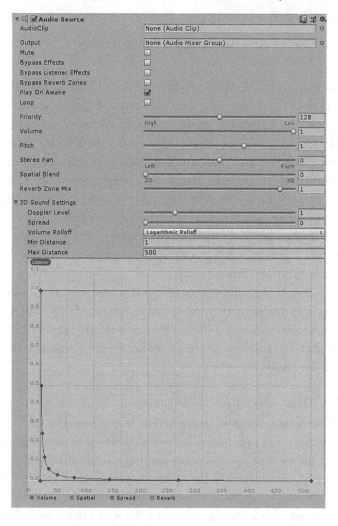

FIGURE 7.2   The AudioSource Component.

camera or an avatar, hears the sound and, in a roundabout way, sends what it hears out to the speakers. The 3D space is an important factor in how the sound will be played back, with panning, volume, and audio effects being applied along the way.

When you apply an AudioSource Component, it has many different properties that directly affect how the engine will process any sounds it will play. AudioSource properties are as follows:

Property	Function
Audio Clip	Unity refers to sound files as Audio Clips. The Audio Clip is the sound file that will be played from this Audio Source.
Output	Sounds can be output through either an Audio Listener or an Audio Mixer. We will look at Audio Mixers a little further on in this chapter.
Mute	Muting the sound means that you will not be able to hear it, even though it will continue to play silently.
Bypass Effects	The Bypass Effects checkbox offers an easy way to turn all effects on/off. When this is checked, effects such as reverb or any filter effects will not be applied to this Audio Source.
Bypass Listener Effects	Listener effects are normally applied to all of the sounds in a scene, but this checkbox toggles Listener effects on/off for this Audio Source.
Bypass Reverb Zones	This checkbox turns Reverb Zones on or off. Reverb zones are areas you can set in a Scene that will cause any sound played within them to have a reverberation effect applied.
Play On Awake	When this box is checked, the Audio Source will start playing as soon as the scene starts. Otherwise, you will need to start playback of this source manually.
Loop	When the Loop box is checked, sound played from this Audio Source will play repeatedly in a loop.
Priority	Priority decides how important it is that this Audio Source gets played. (Priority: 0 = most important. 256 = least important. Default = 128.) Audio Sources with a higher Priority rating will be cut first whenever too many sound channels are being used at the same time. For endless audio, such as music or perhaps ambient background sound, you should use a higher Priority. Unity recommends using 0 for music, so that it will not be interrupted when too many sounds are playing at the same time.
Volume	Volume amount determines at what volume the Audio Source should play the Audio Clip. That is, the volume it should sound like within one world unit (one meter) from the Listener. Volume is usually affected by distance rolloff, meaning that the sound will get quieter the further away the Listener is from it.
Pitch	You can change the pitch (speed) of playback here. The default is 1, which plays the AudioClip at its original pitch.

(Continued)

Property	Function
Stereo Pan	This value influences the left/right panning of the sound. The panning set here is applied before any of the regular 3D panning calculations are carried out. Values range from −1.0 to 1.0, where −1.0 is full left, 0 is centered, and 1.0 is full right.
Spatial Blend	The 3D engine determines the volume and speaker positions of sounds, based on the positional differences between the Audio Source and the Audio Listener. Spatial Blend determines how much the 3D engine affects this Audio Source. If you wanted a 2D sound that will appear everywhere in the Scene, you can set this slider all the way to the left (0). Sliding it all the way to the right will cause the Audio Source to be fully 3D, acting as though it were being emitted from a space in 3D.
Reverb Zone Mix	Sets the amount of the output signal that gets routed to the reverb zones. Unity states that this setting "can be useful to achieve the effect of near-field and distant sounds."
Doppler Level	Determines how much Doppler effect will be applied to sounds played through this Audio Source. See the previous section for a description of the Doppler effect.
Spread	Spread determines how much 3D positioning affects panning of the Audio Source. To visualize this, imagine the space in your left and right speakers and then think of this value as how much of that space will be used by the Audio Clip. If it was set to zero, the sound will come from wherever it is. Anything above zero means that a portion of extra space will be taken up by that sound.
	At zero, full panning occurs based on position. At 180, no panning occurs, but the sound appears to be all the way, right across, from left to right. Setting this to 360 reverses the panning effect, effectively swapping left and right positional panning altogether so that sound objects on the left will sound like they are coming from the right. In most situations, this value would be 0 for sound effects. Use 180 for audio that needs to sound as if it is coming from the whole environment but still needs its audio volume to be affected by distance from the Audio Source in the 3D space (we will use 180 for the ambient audio we will add in the next section).
Min Distance	When the Listener is within MinDistance, the sound coming from this Audio Source will stay at its loudest. When the Listener is outside MinDistance its volume will begin to drop off based on distance.
Max Distance	If the Audio Listener goes beyond Max Distance (units) from the Audio Source, the volume of the sound will stay at its minimum. Unity describes MaxDistance as:
	(Logarithmic rolloff) MaxDistance is the distance a sound stops attenuating at. (Linear rolloff) MaxDistance is the distance where the sound is completely inaudible.
Rolloff Mode	How fast the sound fades. The higher the value, the closer the Listener has to be before hearing the sound. (This is determined by a Graph.)

Now that we have a little background information about the Audio Source Component, we can go ahead and set up our ambient audio in the garden scene.

Adding Audio to the Bug Game

With the project open in Unity, find the Scenes folder and open the scene named game.

Ambient Audio

Ambient sound takes the form of a sound loop that runs in the background of the scene to add a little audio explanation to the location of the action. In the case of a garden, an ambient loop might take the form of birds singing or perhaps a gentle breeze and a nearby lawnmower.

In this section, we add ambient sound to the bug game.

In the Hierarchy pane, expand out the GameController GameObject, then expand out the AudioSources to find the AudioSource_Ambience GameObject. Click AudioSource_Ambience to select it.

In the Inspector, click the Add Component button. Choose Audio > Audio Source.

The Audio Source Component has an AudioClip field at the top of it. To the right of the field is the target icon that lets you choose an audio file. Click the target icon and choose the sound named "garden."

Check the Loop box to make the sound loop over again, then check Play On Awake to make sure that the audio starts automatically at the beginning of the game.

Making ambient audio in Unity demands a specific approach. If you add an Audio Source to a Scene, the sound will appear to be coming from the position of its GameObject. With a regular Audio Source, viewers can walk around it, and it will always appear to be coming from a set location due to panning and fading. For ambience, we need the audio to sound as though it is all around us, rather than being emitted from just a specified point in 3D space.

In the Inspector, on the Audio Source Component attached to AudioSource_Ambience, make sure that Spatial Blend is set to 2D (all the way to the left) (Figure 7.3). In the 3D Sound Settings section (you may need to expand this out, using the small arrow next to the heading) set the Spread level is set to 180.

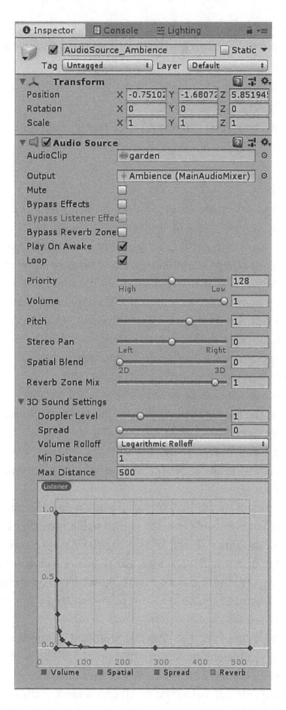

FIGURE 7.3 The AudioSource_Ambience GameObject with its AudioSource Component.

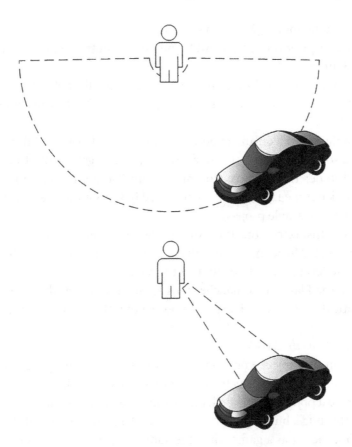

FIGURE 7.4 At the top, a widespread setting (180) makes the car audio sound as though it is coming from all around the Listener. A narrow spread makes the car audio take up less audio space and sounds like it is coming from the direction of the Audio Source.

This will stop the audio from panning around and should make the ambient audio sound as if it is all around the viewer. Spread defines how much audio panning space will be used by this Audio Source (Figure 7.4).

Adding Music

In this section, we add a music track. The procedure is the same as adding an ambient audio track, including removing any panning effects so that it will play as a regular stereo track rather than from an audio source in the 3D world.

In the Hierarchy pane, expand out the GameController GameObject, then expand out the AudioSources and find the AudioSource_Music GameObject.

Click AudioSource_Music to select it.

In the Inspector, click the Add Component button. Choose Audio > Audio Source.

The Audio Source Component has an AudioClip field at the top of it. To the right of the field is the target icon that lets you choose an audio file.

Click the target icon and choose the clip named "Cheerful Annoyance." This is a song from Kenny.nl, an awesome place to get royalty-free assets, licensed under the Creative Commons Zero license. For more information, check out the License text file included in the Sounds/Kenny.nl music folder of the example project.

In the Inspector, on the Audio Source Component attached to AudioSource_Music, make sure that Spatial Blend is set to 2D. Now, set the Spread level (in the 3D Sound Settings section) to 180.

Check the Play On Awake checkbox to make sure that the audio starts automatically. Then, check the Loop box so that the music never ends!

Bringing Life to the World

In the example project, you may have noticed that incoming insects sneak up on you. When the insects are silent like this, they do not seem alive. They are just objects floating silently toward the player. A single audio clip, to give this bug a buzzing sound, can make the scene feel very different. It also works better as a game when the audio gives the player a signal as to where to look.

Insects need to buzz continuously when they fly, and to do that, this Audio Source will use a looping audio. As it gets closer to the Audio Listener (attached to the viewer's camera) the audio will get louder and its position around the viewer's head should become clearer.

Your choice of sound will also affect how easy it is for the player to figure out where the sound is coming from. The brain uses the delay between the sound hitting the ears (known as the phase difference) to figure out the direction of the sound source. A sound with a longer wavelength (a lower pitch sound) helps make this delay between ears easier for the brain to interpret. If you need users to locate the source of the audio, try to choose lower pitched audio or combine high pitched audio with lower pitched audio together. Perhaps people say "moo" instead of "psst!" to subtlety get attention?

You also need to choose sounds that help reinforce the themes of your universe, or whatever it is that is happening in it at the time. Think about the effect you are trying to achieve and how the sound makes you feel. Good sound design uses both direct and indirect communication for effect.

Add Sound to the Insects   Quick note: Prefabs are files that contain GameObjects made up of one or more other GameObjects. The prefabs system is a way to build complex combinations of GameObjects and Components that can be added to the Scene in a single command rather than having to construct them part by part each time you need them. By having a prefab set up for an insect, for example, all we need to do is add an Insect prefab to the game and tell it where to aim. The Insect prefab already has the script Components, physics, and Colliders it needs to function. In this game, a single line of code adds an insect to a Scene, and it is ready to use.

With the example project for this chapter open (Chapter 7—Project 1), in the Project browser, find the Assets/Prefabs folder and click on it so that you can see its contents. Look for the Insect prefab.

Click on Insect in the Project browser, so that you can see its Components and properties in the Inspector.

Click the Open Prefab button (you can also shortcut to this by double clicking on the prefab in the Project browser), then click on the AudioSource_Buzz GameObject in the Hierarchy. This is an empty GameObject parented to the main insect, so it will always appear at the same position in the Scene (note also that its position is set so that the sound comes from the center of the insect).

At the bottom of the Inspector, click Add Component. Choose Audio > Audio Source to add a new Audio Source. On the new Audio Source Component, click on the little target icon next to Audio Clip so that you can choose an Audio Clip to play (Figure 7.5).

Choose the Audio Clip named bzz. Next, check the Loop checkbox so that the sound will play on a loop until either the GameObject is destroyed or we tell it to stop playing.

Drag the Spatial Blend slider all the way to the right so that Spatial Blend is set to 1 (3D). This makes sure that the sound will appear to be coming from the direction of its GameObject.

The last thing you need to do to make this work is to check the Play On Awake checkbox. With Play On Awake checked, whenever an Insect prefab is added to the Scene, the buzzing sound will start to play automatically.

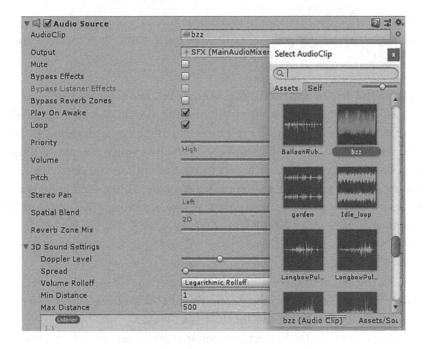

FIGURE 7.5 Choosing an Audio Clip for the Audio Component to play.

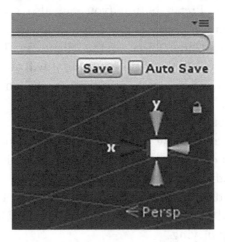

FIGURE 7.6 The Auto Save checkbox and Save button, in the top right of the Scene window.

When you are editing a prefab like this, make sure that the Auto Save checkbox is checked or that, when you are done editing, you click the Save button in the top right of the Scene pane (Figure 7.6). The Auto Save box is there for you to toggle automatic saving on or off whenever you are working on a complicated prefab that takes a while to save. Working on complex prefabs with auto saving happening every time you change a property or move an item can be super frustrating, so remember that you can turn saving on or off as needed!

Press Play and notice how the buzzing sound's volume and panning changes based on its location in the 3D space. You can now hear where the insects are coming from and hopefully spray them before they sting!

Add Sound to the Spray Bottle   When we press the trigger to make spray come out of the spray bottle, it would be nice to make a little sound. The procedure for adding an Audio Clip to the spray is the same as adding audio to the insect in the previous section, but in this section, we will need to add some code to play the audio whenever the spray starts.

In the Project browser, find the Prefabs folder again and, inside that, click on SprayPrefab in the Project browser (in the Prefabs folder). In the Inspector, click the Open Prefab button. It is a complicated Prefab, but if you went through the steps in Chapter 6 to add hand poses to the spray bottle, you should recognize this structure.

In the Inspector, scroll down to the bottom of the Components and click Add Component. Choose Audio > Audio Source. Click on the little target icon next to Audio Clip, so that you can choose the clip named "spray."

This time, we do not need the clip to loop so you can leave that unchecked.

Set the Spatial Blend all the way to 3D, as the spray can is a 3D object we want it to sound like it is coming from the bottle and not from some strange universal place all around.

Save the prefab (click the Save button in the top right of the Scene pane, unless Auto Save is checked, in which case it should save automatically).

Currently, the script we need does not contain any code to play the sound you just added, so we will need to open the code and add it now.

With the SprayPrefab prefab still open for editing and selected, find the Spray Controller (Script) Component in the Inspector and double click in the Script field to open the script. Another way to find this script is to go via the Project browser and find it directly in the Scripts folder, named SprayController.

With the script open in your script editor, you should see something like this:

```
using UnityEngine;
using System.Collections;
using UnityEngine.UI;
using System;


public class SprayController : MonoBehaviour
{

    [Space]
    public Transform _sprayPoint;
    public Transform _sprayColliderPrefab;
    public Transform _sprayParticlePrefab;

    [Space]
    public int ammo = 20;
    public Text _ammoDisplay;
    public LayerMask groundLayerMask;

    void Start()
    {
        _ammoDisplay.text = ammo.ToString("D2");
    }

    public void StartSpray()
    {
        if (ammo <= 0)
            return;

        // decrease ammo and update our display
        ammo--;
        _ammoDisplay.text = ammo.ToString("D2");

        MakeSprayCollider();

        // show spray effect
        Instantiate(_sprayParticlePrefab, _
sprayPoint.position, _sprayPoint.rotation);
    }
```

```
void MakeSprayCollider()
{
        float dist = 2f;
        RaycastHit hit;

        // Does the ray intersect any objects
excluding the player layer
        if (Physics.Raycast(_sprayPoint.position,
_sprayPoint.TransformDirection(Vector3.forward), out
hit, dist, groundLayerMask))
        {
                dist= hit.distance;
        }

        // make invisible collision mesh to hit
bugs with
        Instantiate(_sprayColliderPrefab,
(_sprayPoint.position + _sprayPoint.
TransformDirection(Vector3.forward) * dist),
Quaternion.identity);
    }
}
```

This is the exact same SprayController.cs script from Chapter 6—Advanced Interactions. We are just going to add some extra code here to add audio to it.

Find the end of the variable declarations (just about the Start() function) and add this line, to provide a reference to the sound we want to play:

```
private AudioSource _spraySound;
```

As the Audio Source Component was added to the same GameObject as this script is attached to, we can automatically find the AudioSource Component with the GetComponent() function rather than having to set it through the editor.

At the top of the Start() function, add this:

```
_spraySound = GetComponent<AudioSource>();
```

The GetComponent above will find the first AudioSource attached to the same GameObject and store a reference to it in the variable _spraySound. We can now use this later in the code to tell it to play the audio.

Find the StartSpray() function after this line, which updates the ammo display:

```
_ammoDisplay.text = ammo.ToString("D2");
```

Add this:

```
if (!_spraySound.isPlaying)
     _spraySound.Play();
```

This code starts out by checking the .isPlaying property of the Audio Source, to see if a sound is already being played. As long as this returns false (we don't want to override any currently playing audio), then we can go ahead and call the .Play() function to play the audio clip.

The final script should look like this:

```
using UnityEngine;
using System.Collections;
using UnityEngine.UI;
using System;

public class SprayController : MonoBehaviour
{

     [Space]
     public Transform _sprayPoint;
     public Transform _sprayColliderPrefab;
     public Transform _sprayParticlePrefab;

     [Space]
     public int ammo = 20;
     public Text _ammoDisplay;
     public LayerMask groundLayerMask;

     private AudioSource _spraySound;

     void Start()
     {
          _spraySound = GetComponent<AudioSource>();
          _ammoDisplay.text = ammo.ToString("D2");
     }
```

```
public void StartSpray()
{
        if (ammo <= 0)
              return;


        // decrease ammo and update our display
        ammo--;
        _ammoDisplay.text = ammo.ToString("D2");

        if (!_spraySound.isPlaying)
              _spraySound.Play();

        MakeSprayCollider();


        // show spray effect
        Instantiate(_sprayParticlePrefab, _spray
Point.position, _sprayPoint.rotation);
     }


     void MakeSprayCollider()
     {
        float dist = 2f;
        RaycastHit hit;

        // Does the ray intersect any objects
excluding the player layer
        if (Physics.Raycast(_sprayPoint.position,
_sprayPoint.TransformDirection(Vector3.forward), out
hit, dist, groundLayerMask))
              {
                    dist= hit.distance;
              }

        // make invisible collision mesh to hit
bugs with
        Instantiate(_sprayColliderPrefab, (_spray
Point.position + _sprayPoint.TransformDirection
(Vector3.forward) * dist), Quaternion.identity);
     }
}
```

Now, save (CTRL+S) and return to the Unity editor. After the script has finished recompiling you should be able to press the Play button (grab your headset again!) and hear the spray sound whenever you press the trigger when you are holding a spray bottle.

Mixers

Mixers are used to control the balance between different sounds in your project and to give you greater control over how they are played, as well as to apply effects to groups of sounds. You can use multiple mixers if you need to, but for most small projects, you will likely only need one. Mixers allow you to route audio and control it along its journey to the speakers.

If you have the example project open (Project 1) for this chapter, click on the Sounds folder in the Project browser.

Click the menu Assets > Create > Audio Mixer, to add a new Audio Mixer to the Sounds folder. Name it MainAudioMixer.

Click the menu Window > Audio > Audio Mixer to bring up the Audio Mixer window (Figure 7.7). Before we go on and create anything else, look at the categories in that mixer:

Snapshots

Changing multiple settings would mean that you had to set each property of a Mixer one by one. Snapshots enable you to take a "snapshot" of all settings and save it. You can then choose a snapshot to load. A good example of how you might use this could be the difference between indoor and outdoor vehicle audio. Engine sounds are very different on the outside of the car

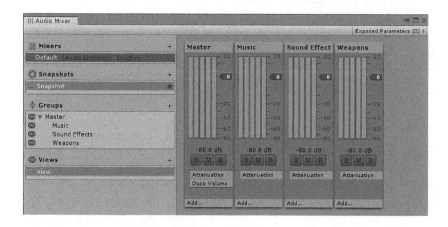

FIGURE 7.7 The Audio Mixer window.

than inside. For this, you could have two Snapshots, one for indoor and the other for outdoor. By applying different effects and levels to the indoor settings, the engine sounds and road noise could be lower with effects applied to make them sound "muffled" as if the sound proofing were doing its job. On the outside Snapshot, the sound could be louder and perhaps with a little more reverb. When the simulation moves from inside the car to outside (such as a camera change, or the viewer physically exiting the vehicle) you could switch to the applicable Snapshot to make the audio sound correct.

Groups

You might think of a Group as an individual channel where you can route whatever sounds you want. By using multiple Groups, you can control the volume and effects applied to whichever sounds you choose to route through them. For example, you might have a Group for sound effects and a Group for music. The music Group could have a different volume to the sound Group so that you can control music and sound volumes individually.

By default, Unity adds a single group named Master to every Mixer, and I usually add new Groups that are children of the Master so that whenever settings are changed on the Master group, they carry down to the others. For example, to create a master volume controller slider for an options menu, the master needs to affect all volume levels. Changing the volume level on the Master affects the volume on any child Groups, so to create a master volume slider I would make all my sound effect and music Groups children of the Master Group so that they would all be affected by the settings applied to the Master. Like most object systems in Unity, it is hierarchical.

Views

Views are there to help you work with Groups. By using the little eye icons next to each group, you can choose which groups are showing for you to edit in the Audio Mixer window. Views enable you to automate the process of using those eye icons. For example, you could set up a View to show only one set of groups such as those associated with vehicle audio. Another View might be used to only show nature sounds. When you are working with many Groups, the View system will help you work more efficiently with them all.

Setting Up Mixers in the Audio Mixer Window

Audio Groups are shown on the right of the window as channels (Figure 7.8). Whenever sound is being played through the Group you will see the volume unity (VU) meter showing levels. The dark gray arrow to

FIGURE 7.8   Click the + icon to add Groups to the Audio Mixer.

the right of the VU meter is moveable with the mouse, and it points to the currently set attenuation level on this channel. The default is 0 dB. This will affect how loud the sound will be output.

Below the VU meter you will find three icon buttons: S, M, and B. Those are (in order)

Solo (S): This will mute audio through any other Groups that are not currently soloed. That is, you will only hear the audio flowing through this Group, and all other audio Groups will be silent (unless they are also set to be soloed by having their S button highlighted). When you have a lot of Groups, this is useful to be able to isolate a single Group when balancing and tweaking audio settings.

Mute (M): The mute button will mute all audio going through this Group. Other Groups will continue to behave as normal.

Bypass (B): If effects have been applied to this Group, the Bypass button will bypass the effects system and play the audio dry. This button only applies to the current Group. If there are any parent or child Groups connected to it, they will not be affected. Only the current Group's effects will be bypassed by this button.

At the bottom of the Group mixer, you can add or modify effects. I will not be going into any detail over this part, as it is a varied and complex subject that is beyond the scope of this chapter. If you need more in-depth information on the effects and audio system, the Unity documentation is a good place to start.

Adding Mixer Groups

Click the + button in the top right of the Groups section. Add three new Groups and name them SFX, Ambience, and Music so that it looks like those in Figure 7.9.

Make sure that all the new groups are under the Master Group. You can change their order by dragging and dropping them in this area if you

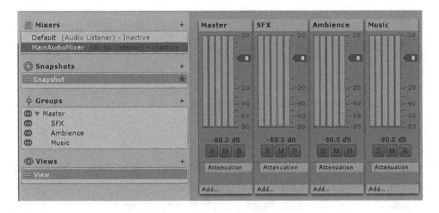

FIGURE 7.9   The Audio Mixers for the insect game.

need to. By having the SFX, Music, and Ambience groups beneath the Master, whenever we change the master volume all our other sounds will also be affected by the change.

Setting Audio Sources to Use the Audio Mixer Groups

Now that we have an Audio Mixer and it has groups set up for sound effects and music, we need to go ahead and tell the Audio Sources to use them. These are the Audio Sources added as Components to GameObjects earlier in this chapter. The audio will work even without any Audio Mixer setup, but its output will just go direct to the Listener. Routing output via the Mixer provides global control from a single place.

Start by setting up the ambience. In the Hierarchy, click the GameController GameObject to expand it out. Find and click on the AudioSource_Ambience GameObject. In the Inspector, find the Audio Source Component and click on the little target icon next to the Output.

When the Audio Mixers list pops up, choose Ambience (under MainAudioMixer).

Next, the sound effects. In the Hierarchy, find AudioSource_Ouch. In the Inspector, find the Audio Source Component and click on the little target icon next to Output. Set the Output to SFX (under MainAudioMixer).

Remember that the insects have sound effects too. In the Project browser, find the Prefabs folder and double click on the Insect prefab (alternatively, click on it once and choose the Open Prefab button in the Inspector). It contains:

Insect

    Frame1

    Frame2

    AudioSource_Buzz

    AudioSource_Hit

When an insect spawns, the sound AudioSource_Buzz loops. When an insect is sprayed, the AudioSource_Hit plays.

Click the AudioSource_Buzz prefab in the Project browser. In the Inspector, under Audio Source, set the Output to SFX.

Click the AudioSource_Hit prefab. Again, in the Inspector, Audio Source, set the Output to SFX.

The SprayPrefab prefab is the last thing we need to set up. Click SprayPrefab in the Prefabs folder and set its Output to SFX on the Audio Source Component.

Testing and Mixing Audio

Unity's audio system provides a strong interface for editing and setting up audio. You can see audio levels in real time and even apply audio effects as the audio is playing live. Mixing is done through the Audio Mixer window (as we saw back in the Adding Mixer Groups section of this chapter).

When you try out the preview, the first thing you might notice is how much more alive it seems. The ambient audio helps to reinforce the garden visual and, as insects appear, you can hear them approach and know where they are coming from. The insects have character too. When you spray them, they make a cute little "bzzt" sound as they fly away. The pitch-shifted voice makes it sound small and cute, taking a little more away from the potentially dark theme of spraying bugs. As the bugs never die, they just fly away, the tone is happy and light. Our audio adds to this, taking a lighthearted and fun approach to the garden invaders scenario.

Do not be afraid to experiment. One of the top sound designers in Hollywood, Skip Lievsay, once said that he uses the sound of bacon sizzling for rain sound effects, and he mixes lion roars in with car engines to make them more aggressive (Kisner, 2015). It is not just about the sound, but the kind of feeling that a sound evokes when you hear it. For example, perhaps you need a creaky door in a haunted house VR experience. The door needs to creak and all the doors in your house do not creak, so you cannot use them. Instead, you could recreate the effect in a sound editor package by sequencing three sounds one after the other. The first sound is the door handle rattle as it is turned. Stage two is the little click sound of the latch opening. The final stage is the creak, which could be recorded from a creaky drawer instead or perhaps something unrelated such as bending a piece of wood to make a creaking sound. The listener may never know that it was not a real creaking door sound used in the haunted house, but the effect could be unforgettable when they hear a creepy old door opening, and they wonder what is going to walk through it! Get creative with sound to create more than just a copy of a sound to something that will help create the atmosphere you want.

We create universes, with their own rules and physics, creatures, and architecture. It is important to try to reinforce not just the visual environment but the themes and tone of the whole experience. By considering more than what is immediately visible, we build a richer and more complete universe for the player to inhabit.

Audio Effects

Audio Ducking   Audio Ducking is an effect commonly used by audio engineers to bring down the volume of an audio track so that another audio track is easier to hear. Unity includes a built-in audio ducking effect that we can easily apply to a mixer.

In the Sounds folder of the Project browser, find and double click on the Mixer named MainAudioMixer (the one you added earlier in this chapter). In the Audio Mixer window, you should see the three groups: Master, SFX, Ambience, and Music.

At the bottom of each mixer group is the Add.button, for Effects.

Send and Receive   Mixer channels (groups) can send and receive data to each other. For audio ducking, the mixer channel you want to have affected by ducking must receive audio from another channel. We will have the Music channel duck based on the output of the SFX channel, so the first thing to do is to add a Send effect to SFX.

In the Audio Mixer view, at the bottom of Music click the Add button and choose Duck Volume. No, this has nothing to do with quacking.

At the bottom of the SFX channel, click Add and choose Send. Over in the Inspector, with the SFX channel selected, you should now see a

Send Component. Here, we need to tell Send where its data should be received. Click on the Receive dropdown (in the Inspector) and choose Music\Duck Volume.

The Send level, also in the Inspector, is important because it determines how "loud" the output from this channel should be sent to its receiver. Slide the Send level all the way to the right, until the number to the right of the slider reads 0.00 dB.

Audio Ducking Settings   To get the most satisfactory effect from audio ducking, you will usually need to do a little tweaking of the values it uses to determine how much input audio it takes for ducking to happen and how it will duck. Guessing these values would be beyond difficult, so Unity has provided a method of setting up the audio as the preview is running so that you get a live audioscape to play around with, and you can immediately experience the effect that the settings changes are having.

When you hit Play to preview the scene, the audio views gray out to tell you that you cannot do anything with them in play mode. Additionally, in play mode, two new toggle buttons appear atop the Audio Mixer view and at the top of the Inspector when you have an audio channel selected—both are labeled "Edit in Play Mode."

Click the Edit in Play Mode when the preview is running and you can change any or all the audio values and contrary to normal Unity operation, the changes will persist after you hit the Stop button to return to editing.

Through trial and error, I went through setting up values as I listened to how the buzzing noise got louder as an insect approached the player and then how the audio ducking affected the volume of the music. I ended up changing the following values:

Threshold: −27.50

Attack Time: 583.00

Note that in the Inspector, you can drag the white line left or right over the visual representation (Figure 7.10) to set the Threshold. If you press Play to preview, the graph will show the audio input and you will see where the Threshold kicks in versus where the audio levels are from the input.

You can get a good measure of the Threshold by using the graph.

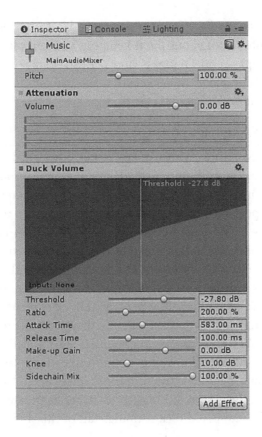

FIGURE 7.10   Audio Ducking settings are set in the Inspector.

Try Out the Audio

Grab your headset, controllers, headphones—everything you need to test this out. What you should hear is that the music plays on a loop along with the ambient sound. The insects start out quiet but you hear them as they approach. The Audio Ducking effect makes the music quieten down whenever the game sound effects are loud, so as a bug approaches the music quietens to let you hear the sound effects more.

Getting all the sounds at the correct volumes, setting up effects like Audio Ducking and reverb are all things that take time and skill to put together effectively. Make sure to set aside some production time for mixing all your audio together once it is all in your project.

Oh, and well done! You just added sounds to the game!

Other Effects   Just a quick mention of these, as we have been so close to them all. At the bottom of the audio groups in the Audio Mixer, you can find a host of other audio effects inside the Add button dropdown menu. I will not go into detail about them here, but you can play around with things like Lowpass and Highpass filters, Echo, Flange, and Distortion effects—all sorts of really cool effects that you can add to different audio groups for a number of different effects.

USING STEAM AUDIO FOR VR

Separate from SteamVR, Valve offers something called Steam Audio, which can be used to add more realistic audio to your project. Although it is separate from SteamVR, the quality of audio can complement a VR experience—especially when surround headphones are in use.

The best way I can describe what Steam Audio does is with a little imaginary scenario. Try to imagine that you are in a basement. The stairs curve around, out of the basement and up behind a wall. Now imagine that someone is talking to you from upstairs. What you hear from the basement is kind of muffled. The person walks down the stairs toward the basement, and as they make their way they continue to talk and the sound changes. As they approach, the sound is less muffled but when they are behind the wall it still does not sound quite clear. It sounds a little phased, as the sound waves bounce off the surfaces and make their way to your ear. Finally, the person talking arrives in the basement and the audio sounds normal. Steam Audio can simulate all of this and make it sound true to life.

Adding the Steam Audio API to Unity

Open the example project for this chapter, Chapter 7—Project 2—Steam Audio. Find and open the Scene named main (in the Assets folder).

As a side note, this project contains a basic indoor environment (Figure 7.11) that you can teleport around to hear the difference Steam Audio makes. To make this environment quickly, I used ProBuilder, a 3D modeling package built right into Unity. Installing ProBuilder is as simple as going to Window > PackageManager, finding ProBuilder, and clicking the Install button. I will not be covering ProBuilder in this book, but I will say that it is a great way to block out environments quickly for small test projects like this. It is also capable of modeling fully textured 3D environments and props.

Grab your headset (and headphones, if needed) and press Play in the editor to give it a try. Right now, the project allows you to teleport around the environment by pressing the trackpad down. Teleport your way into

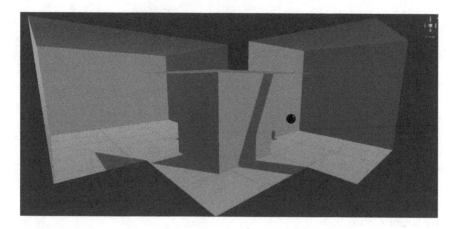

FIGURE 7.11 The example projects 3D environment, for testing spatial audio.

the next room and notice how the audio volume gets lower as you get further away from the audio source (shown as a 3D sphere).

So, the audio volume changes based on distance, but the actual sound remains the same. If this was a real scenario, as you moved through the corridor and into another room, the sound would change based on how the sound waves bounce off the walls on the way to your ears. In this section, we will add Steam Audio to simulate that effect and make the audio sound more realistic.

Download Steam Audio
Download Steam Audio for Unity from https://valvesoftware.github.io/steam-audio/downloads.html.

Choose Unity Package as the download. Once the download has finished, extract the zip file. In the folder steamaudio_unity/bin/unity, you should find the SteamAudio.unitypackage file. With the example project still open in the background, double click this.unitypackage file.

Unity should open the package and offer to extract it into the project. Click the Import button to have Unity import the Steam Audio files.

Next, you need to select Steam Audio as Unity's spatializer plugin.

Click Edit > Project Settings > Audio. (Figure 7.12)

Next to Spatializer Plugin is a dropdown. Click the dropdown and choose Steam Audio Spatializer.

Click the Ambisonic Decoder Plugin dropdown and choose Steam Audio Ambisonics.

FIGURE 7.12 The Project Settings Audio window, spatial and ambionic settings for Steam Audio.

Set Up the Level for Steam Audio

For Steam Audio to work, each Scene needs a Steam Audio Manager object. This will be created for you after the next step.

Click the menu Window > Steam Audio.

Your Scene should now have a Steam Audio Manager GameObject in it (named Steam Audio Manager Settings).

In the Audio Engine dropdown, make sure that it is selected to Unity. You can also choose to use the FMOD audio system, but we will not be covering FMOD in this book. Only Unity.

In the Hierarchy, find the GameObject named ROOMS. This GameObject contains the room 3D model. As Steam Audio will need to calculate the properties of the sound based on the environment, we need to add a Steam Audio Geometry Component to tell Steam Audio what models in the Scene make up the environment we want it to use for its calculations.

With the ROOMS GameObject still selected in the Hierarchy, in the Inspector, click Add Component. Choose Steam Audio Geometry (remember that if you cannot find it easily in the list, you can use the search bar at the top of the window to go straight to it). The Steam Audio Geometry Component has no configurable properties, but instead it displays vertex and triangle count for the model it has processed.

Steam Audio Materials

The way sound waves bounce depends on the types of surface it is bouncing off. For example, a hard metal surface is less likely to dull the reflected wave than a carpeted wall. For that reason, for a realistic audio simulation we need to tell Steam Audio about the surface of our geometry. We do this with a Steam Audio Material.

In the Inspector, click Add Component again (with the ROOMS object still selected) and choose Steam Audio Material. The dropdown shows all the available materials, such as Generic, Brick, Concrete, Ceramic, Gravel, Carpet, Glass, Plaster, Wood, Metal, Rock, and Custom.

Choose Metal from the Dropdown

In this example, we are only choosing one material for the entire environ-ment. In a production case, you would separate out the floor and ceil-ing from the walls and choose the correct material for each one. For now, though, the single material will be enough for this purpose.

Setting Up an Audio Source for Steam Audio

Each Audio Source in your Scene needs a Steam Audio Source Component for it to work with Steam Audio. The original Unity Audio Source Component will also need to be set up for spatialization.

In the Hierarchy, find the SOUNDEMITTER GameObject and click on it to highlight it.

Click Add Component in the Inspector. Choose Steam Audio Source.

Now that we have the Component, we need to tell the regular Audio Source Component to use custom spatialization (think of this as rout-ing the audio through the Steam Audio spatializer rather than playing through the normal Unity audio channels).

Near the top of the Audio Source Component, find the Spatialization checkbox (Figure 7.13) and check it.

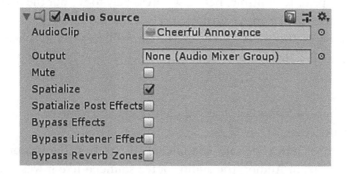

FIGURE 7.13 The Audio Source Component needs to be set to use custom spatialization for the audio to play through Steam Audio.

Reflection

In the real world, sound waves bounce around off the walls, the ceiling, the floor—all over the place. To simulate the effect, Steam Audio can apply physics-based environmental effects to an Audio Source. We want to hear what this sounds like in our Scene, so let's set it up here.

Click on the SOUNDEMITTER GameObject in the Scene. In the Inspector, find the Steam Audio Source Component. Under the Indirect Sound heading, check the Reflections checkbox to enable reflections.

With the Scene and level geometry set up and the audio emitter ready to go, we can now go ahead and tell Steam Audio to calculate the data it needs to function.

Precalculating the Steam Audio Scene

Steam Audio is designed to be as efficient as possible, utilizing multicore processing, and threading to distribute the processing load as evenly as possible. There is, however, always going to be a performance cost for the processing it takes to produce truly realistic audio. If you have a lot of audio sources and complex geometry, that is when you may start to see performance affected negatively. Many audio sources, such as incidental sounds played close to the user, may not even benefit from the advanced audio system enough to justify the performance hit. Consider how the sound will be used in the environment and whether it needs to be a part of the Steam Audio system before setting it up. Try to avoid many moving sounds and utilize static sounds with Steam Audio, instead.

To help stop overloading the CPU (central processing unit) with audio processing, Steam Audio precalculates a lot of the data it needs for the geometry prior to runtime. Before we press Play to try out the Scene, you should calculate Steam Audio data.

Click on the Steam Audio Manager GameObject in the Scene. In the Inspector, click Pre-Export Scene.

Test the Scene

Right. Grab your headset, tracked controllers and your headphones and hit Play in the editor!

Remember how the Scene sounded at the start of this section, before we added Steam Audio? The audio source sounded like it was close, but now it sounds like it is in the room with you. Move around by teleporting (right trackpad) and make your way down the corridor to the other room.

Notice how the audio sounds as you move—it is much more realistic than standard audio.

We have only just scratched the surface here as to what Steam Audio can do for your audio. I strongly suggest reading through the documentation online at https://valvesoftware.github.io/steam-audio/doc/phonon_unity.html#setting-up-your-unity-project.

QUICK VR AUDIO DESIGN TIPS

Try not to overwhelm your users with too many sounds. For some, VR is already an overload for the senses—try to make sure that the main parts of your simulation have the focus of the audio, and lower priority items have sounds that blend into the background and do not compete with your main sounds. Try out some different pitch ranges, volume ranges, and spatial amounts to achieve effects that will reinforce themes without turning into a wall of noise.

If things are happening that the user may not be looking out (out of their view) and you intend to highlight them using sound, choose a sound that is easy to locate and will stand out to get their attention when there are a lot of other sounds happening at the same time.

Prioritize your sounds in order of how important it is that they are heard. Try to adjust volumes, pitch, and how much they stand out, to help sounds blend in a hierarchical manner that matches your priority list.

Test your sounds in VR, inside the headsets, headphones, or whichever audio device is most commonly going to be used by your users. The way the audio sounds, blends, and works in each scene will be different and, if viewers can move around, should be experienced from several different positions to get the full picture of how they work.

If you have a sound engineer, allow them regular access to VR to try out the sounds. They will experience and hear things differently to experiencing them on a regular screen.

Use music to help bring your environment together and to add atmosphere.

Keep music to a stereo track and avoid using spatialized audio for music. Spatialized music will confuse other spatialized sound and make it harder for users to know where sounds are coming from.

Avoid sounds that are obviously looping. Any kind of crackle or short looped sounds will be annoying to the user and even more obvious than normal when experienced in VR.

Be aware of any distortion, popping, or "broken" audio files. In VR—especially in good VR headphones—audio mistakes are much more obvious than through regular speakers and can break immersion.

RECAP

This chapter was all about audio. We began by looking at setting up audio in Unity and what properties needed to be set specifically for VR. The properties of the AudioSource were key to making this work. We looked at Audio Mixers, how to set them up, and how you can use them to route audio on its way to the speakers. After looking at standard Unity audio, the Steam Audio system gave us a taste of a high-end audio processing system. Although we have only just scratched the surface, there should have been enough in this chapter for you to produce audio for your VR experiences at a professional level. In the next chapter, we will explore the options available for setting up the camera and play area for seated or room-scale experiences.

CHAPTER 8

Building Seated or Static VR Experiences

I MAGINE A VIRTUAL RACING CAR DRIVER SITTING IN THE SEAT OF A virtual racing car. Their head is resting against the headrest in the virtual world. This means that the camera rig, in the Unity Scene, starts out positioned where the virtual racing driver's vision would be. In the real world, when we start the race, the player's head position may not be in the right place for this to line up. By resetting the view and setting Steam virtual reality (SteamVR) tracking to a seated configuration, the Unity camera will be oriented to player's view without changing the camera's position in the 3D Scene. After a reset, the viewer's head will match the virtual racing driver's viewpoint. That is, the camera will start out in the right place for driving.

A SEATED EXPERIENCE

In this section, we look at a seated configuration. The example project will have viewers sit on a chair inside a little house. Thanks to my son, Will, for building the house in MagicaVoxel for me!

Open the Example Project

Open the example Unity project for this chapter—Chapter 8—Project 1. In the Project browser, find the Scenes folder and, inside that, double click the Scene named main to open it in Unity.

When you look at the camera in the Game View, you can see that the camera is correctly located at a position around the viewpoint of a person sitting on the chair, but without any code to tell SteamVR to do anything different, the VR view would start out in a different position. By default, the view can start anywhere in the entire VR play area depending on wherever the headset is at the time. For a seated experience, we need to tell the tracking system to start off in a fixed location, instead. In this example, a script named VR_Config.cs takes care of that. We will look at the script in detail in the next section, but for now grab your headset and press Play in the editor. You should start out in the correct place, facing the right way. If not, press the R key on the keyboard to recenter to view correctly.

SETTING SITTING OR STANDING CALIBRATION IN CODE

We can choose SteamVR's tracking mode via the SteamVR_Render class. It is a Singleton, which means we can access it via SteamVR_Render. instance from anywhere in the code. In this section, we build a simple script Component that will set SteamVR to sitting or standing, depending on which one you choose in the Inspector. With a seated experience, it is also important to provide the functionality for recentering the view whenever the viewer presses a button or key on the keyboard. The most common reason for resetting is that sometimes the viewer is not quite in the right position when the simulation starts. Perhaps they were still putting the headset on after loading the simulation, for example. When that happens, the default position is incorrect for their headset and it needs to be reset.

Click on the [CameraRig] GameObject in the Hierarchy.

With [CameraRig] highlighted, in the Inspector you should see a script named VR_Config. Right click the Component in the Inspector and choose Edit Script from the menu to open it in your script editor. It looks like this:

```
using UnityEngine;
using System.Collections;
using Valve.VR;


public class VR_Config : MonoBehaviour
{
    public enum roomTypes { standing, sitting };
```

```
public roomTypes theRoomType;

void Awake()
{
    SetUpRoom();
}

void SetUpRoom()
{
    if (theRoomType == roomTypes.standing)
    {
            SteamVR_Settings.instance.
trackingSpace= ETrackingUniverseOrigin.
TrackingUniverseStanding;
        }
    else
    {
            SteamVR_Settings.instance.
trackingSpace = ETrackingUniverseOrigin.
TrackingUniverseSeated;
    }

    Recenter();
}

void LateUpdate()
{
    // here, we check for a keypress to reset the
view
    // whenever the mode is sitting .. don't
forget to set this up in Input Manager
    if (theRoomType == roomTypes.sitting)
    {
        if (Input.GetKeyUp(KeyCode.R))
        {
            Recenter();
        }
    }
}

void Recenter()
{
```

```
        // reset the position
        var system = OpenVR.System;
        if (system != null)
        {
            system.ResetSeatedZeroPose();
        }
    }
}
```

Script Breakdown

```
using UnityEngine;
using System.Collections;
using Valve.VR;
```

Above, we need to tell Unity about Valve.VR because SteamVR_Render is a part of the Valve.VR packages included as part of the SteamVR library.

Next up, we see the class declaration:

```
public class VR_Config : MonoBehaviour
{
    public enum roomTypes { standing, sitting };
    public roomTypes theRoomType;
```

The class derives from MonoBehaviour, which we need to do so that we can tap into the Awake() and Update() functions called automatically by the engine.

After the class declaration, we declare an enumeration (a set of constants) to represent a state of either standing or sitting. You could add as many states as you want between the curly brackets, but for this example, we only need the two. Note that all enumerations (enums) are types—this means there is no concept of static or nonstatic, but you will be able to access enums as though they are static from any other part of your code.

The variable theRoomType utilizes the enumeration from the previous line. By making theRoomType a public variable, when it appears in the Inspector inside Unity, the field will appear as a dropdown containing whatever we put into those curly brackets for roomTypes—in this case, we will see a dropdown containing standing and sitting.

The next section of code is the Awake() function, where we call another function to set up the room:

```
void Awake()
{
    SetUpRoom();
}
```

The Awake() function calls to SetUpRoom(), rather than having any of the actual setup code in the Awake function itself. You may wonder why we do not put the code in the Awake() function. Well, splitting code out into separate functions like this is good practice—if we ever need to call our SetUpRoom() code more than once, or from another place, we can easily do that when it is encased in its own function rather than inside Awake().

That brings us to the next function in our class, SetUpRoom():

```
void SetUpRoom()
    {
        if (theRoomType == roomTypes.standing)
        {
                SteamVR_Settings.instance.
trackingSpace= ETrackingUniverseOrigin.
TrackingUniverseStanding;
        }
        else
        {
                SteamVR_Settings.instance.
trackingSpace = ETrackingUniverseOrigin.
TrackingUniverseSeated;
        }

        Recenter();
    }
```

SetUpRoom() tells SteamVR which type of tracking we are going to be using. Based on the value of theRoomType, we talk to the (Singleton) instance of SteamVR_Settings to tell it how to deal with tracking space.

ETrackingUniverseOrigin has three possible values:

TrackingUniverseRawAndUncalibrated: This setting is not calibrated for either standing or sitting. What happens regarding the space and how the view interacts with it, under this setting, may be unpredictable. Valve recommends that TrackingUniverseRawAndUncalibrated should be avoided.

TrackingUniverseSeated: Using the TrackingUniverseSeated setting means that SteamVR will function a lot better with the kinds of positions and movements, which happen in a seated position. Unlike some native VR setups, there is no specific seated calibration in the SteamVR setup procedure (when you first set up the headset in SteamVR and configured the space). If the system is calibrated to room scale, it will intelligently figure out seated parameters as required. Also note that the seated setting does not "lock" the player into place, but instead uses settings that are more suited to a seated position. You will still be able to get up and walk away from the seated position and it is up to the developer to solve this issue, if you need to (for example, pausing the simulation if the player steps too far away from the center point or blacking out the view when they leave a small play area).

TrackingUniverseStanding: SteamVR will use the standing settings, which are more suited to standing or room-scale VR experiences.

After the tracking type is set, there is a quick call to Recenter() that will make sure the view in the headset matches up with the fixed camera position in VR. We will look at Recenter() a little further down in the code. Before we get to that, it is the LateUpdate() function:

```
void LateUpdate()
{
    // here, we check for a keypress to reset the
view
    // whenever the mode is sitting
    if (theRoomType == roomTypes.sitting)
    {
        if (Input.GetKeyUp(KeyCode.R))
        {
            Recenter();
        }
    }
}
```

LateUpdate() is a function called automatically by Unity at the end of every update cycle. LateUpdate is a great place to grab user input—Unity recommends to do keyboard input checks here.

We only need check for a recenter key hit when the room type is sitting. After the check to make sure the script is set to "sitting" mode, we look for the up state of the R key like this:

```
if (Input.GetKeyUp(KeyCode.R))
```

If R has just been pressed and released, GetKeyUp returns true and we are good to call the Recenter() function at the user's request, which is the next function in the class:

```
void Recenter()
{

    // reset the position
    var system = OpenVR.System;
    if (system != null)
    {
```

Recenter() is another local function intended only to be called from within the VR_Config class.

Above, we start out with a locally scoped variable (i.e. a variable that only exists inside this function) named system, to store a reference to OpenVR.System.

OpenVR is another class belonging to the Valve.VR namespace. It provides several system-level commands and properties such as resetting the view and accessing some other hardware features.

If the variable system is null, we know that OpenVR has not initialized correctly. If there has been any sort of problem during the initialization of the OpenVR class, we do this quick null check to keep Unity from throwing an error. Null checking like this can avoid errors, but sometimes you may also want to handle them—you should always be careful not to hide a problem this way rather than solve it (say, for example, if OpenVR was broken we wouldn't know because the null check makes sure we never see any error about it). In this case, we should be safe to assume that if an error occurs with OpenVR initialization that SteamVR will report it to us in another part of the code. I just wanted to mention the danger of null checking as a side note, so always be aware that null checking should be used a little carefully. Another option for safe null checks is to include a message to the Debug.Log() that will report out the log whenever the state is found to be null.

Once we know that OpenVR is ready:

```
            system.ResetSeatedZeroPose();
        }
    }
```

The command to reset the view is system.ResetSeatedZeroPose(). When this is called, the view will immediately reset to the original position and orientation of the camera inside your Unity Scene.

MOVING AROUND INSIDE A VEHICLE

The procedure for sitting a virtual visitor in a vehicle is straightforward. Essentially, you are going to be parenting the camera to the vehicle. Unlike videogames, we need the camera to remain in a fixed position relative to the vehicle. This is contrary to common methods for attaching cameras to vehicles in videogames. Videogames often employ a technique where the player's viewpoint is attached to physics spring so that it moves around as though the player's body or head movement is affected by the movement of the vehicle. In VR, this would be a surefire ticket to making our players ill and should be avoided.

Try the Example Project

Open the example project for this chapter, Chapter 8—Project 2—Vehicle. In the Project browser, find the Scene named main, inside the Scenes folder, and double click it to open.

Look for the Vehicle GameObject in the Hierarchy and click the little arrow next to it, to expand it out and see all child objects.

One of the children of Vehicle is an empty GameObject named CameraMount. This GameObject is positioned where the driver's head should start—at the top of the seat, looking forward to the front of the vehicle. Click on the arrow next to CameraMount and you will see the standard [CameraRig] Prefab object from SteamVR. It is parented to the CameraMount so that it will move and rotate around with the vehicle. The only difference between the regular [CameraRig] and this one is the addition of the VR_Config Component we scripted in the previous section of this chapter.

The vehicle could be just about anything you want the viewer to ride or follow. For example, it could be a carriage of a moving train, a seat on a motorbike, and so forth.

Preview the Scene

Grab your headset and press Play to preview the scene, but if you are at all susceptible to VR sickness, I recommend that you keep your time in this simulation down to a shorter period, just in case this type of movement is uncomfortable. In the next chapter, we will discuss this further and investigate methods to reduce sickness-causing symptoms or to provide comfort options for our users.

RECAP

In this chapter, we looked at the taking control of the camera away from the viewer and relocating it to a fixed place in the virtual world. By modifying the tracking mode, cameras appear where we want instead of their positioning being based on its position in the room-scale VR space. We also looked at the importance of having a recenter button to reset the view for a seated viewer whenever the calibration was out of sync with our simulated viewpoint.

We sat in a room, which was spectacular fun. We also looked at moving around inside a vehicle. Although it was a ground-based vehicle, the principle would be the same for flying water or space-based vehicles too. Essentially, parenting the camera rig to your vehicle is the way to go. We then saved our work (yes, I am sure you have gotten the message now about saving your work regularly, but I will continue to push the issue!). Put the kettle on and get ready for a bit of theory; In the next chapter, we investigate VR sickness and some of the research that has gone into figuring it all out. Hopefully, this information will help us all to make more comfortable and accessible experiences for a wider range of virtual visitors.

CHAPTER 9

Virtual Reality Sickness

I F YOU ARE BUILDING VIRTUAL REALITY (VR), it may be a benefit to understand how much of an issue VR sickness currently is and why. There is a lot of misinformation. VR sickness is something that could seriously inhibit widespread adoption. At such an early stage in VR evolution, we are all ambassadors for the virtual world, and our experiences may very well help to shape its future. It is every VR content creator's responsibility to try to lessen or find workarounds for VR sickness if we are going to see this generation of VR succeed.

This chapter is not about forcing anyone to build VR experiences in a particular way, or even saying that you should not create experiences that may make people feel ill. Honestly, if you want to go ahead and target the groups of people who are not affected by sickness, you should go ahead and do that because there will be people who can enjoy it without an issue. On the other hand, providing options to turn on or off sickness prevention systems could be a great selling point for your game, and we need to understand that everyone is different and people are affected in different ways by VR sickness. For that reason, I am providing problems and solutions in this chapter so that you may consider the options and take what you want from them.

Room-scale VR experiences do not suffer from the same kinds of simulation sickness problems as seated or automated moving experiences. If you do intend to automate movement or gaze in any way, this chapter will help you to know what you are up against.

This chapter is text-heavy. I have tried to collect my findings, through various research papers, websites, articles, and conversations, into something more readable than academic. I want to give you as full a picture as possible into why we think these things are happening to our virtual visitors and you will come away from this book with both theoretical and practical methods to make VR experiences more comfortable. I begin by asking the most obvious question.

WHAT IS VR SICKNESS?

VR sickness is also known as simulator sickness or cyber sickness. It can manifest as a range of symptoms like sweating, nausea, sickness, headaches, and drowsiness, and other symptoms like those experienced by motion sickness sufferers who get sick in cars, boats, or planes.

Despite years of research, we still do not know exactly what causes it. The most popular theory is that VR sickness is caused by a mismatch between what a viewer experiences versus what the viewer's brain thinks it is experiencing. This is known as cue conflict theory (Kolansinski, 1995). Cue conflict theory is when the brain thinks that the input (sight, sound, and so on) is not real or correct. Our minds perform "safety checks" to make sure that the body is in a healthy state. The detection system looks for cues or clues to abnormalities, such as tying movement and sight together to build up a body of information to confirm that what you are experiencing is correct. When the cues do not match up, the brain switches into a defensive mode. This mode would normally be triggered when the body is under threat from poison or a similar attack. A rejection system kicks in as the brain attempts to rid the body of any poisons, through bodily fluid (sweat secretion and/or vomiting depending on severity).

PERSONAL EXPERIENCE

The first VR development kit I used made me feel sick within minutes of using it. The sickness would last anything from a few hours or right up to a full day after taking off the headset. I began to wonder if I would ever be able to stay inside the headset for more than just a few moments at a time. And it just seemed to get harder and harder. Over time, it was as if my brain started to associate the headset with feeling sick. I hardly needed to switch it on before the symptoms kicked in and even the smell of the headset plastic would make me start to feel ill. The word from some researchers is that you can build up a tolerance to VR sickness over time, which is what people commonly refer to as "finding your VR legs," but that never happened to me and I have since spoken to several other developers whose tolerance never got any better. Despite starting small, every day spending short bursts of time in VR, I was never able to extend my time. I also tried travel sickness meds and homeopathic treatment. After months of trying, I decided to skip the next development kit and wait for the consumer versions to see if any significant improvements would have been made. And, thankfully, they had.

The difference was amazing between the Rift development kit 1 (DK1) and the consumer headsets. I still struggle with some types of movement, and there are some games that can put me out for a long time, but there are many more VR experiences I can play now with little or no sickness at all.

My own experiences led me to believe that the technical aspects—primitive resolution display and slower refresh rates of the development kit—could have been the main contributors to my discomfort. Many researchers agree, but we need to be careful about making assumptions which rely on our own experiences. Not everyone is affected in the same way.

VR SICKNESS SYMPTOMS AND CUES

VR visitors are affected in different ways and by different situations. Some people exhibit all the signs and symptoms, whereas others only experience a few or none. Kennedy and Fowlkes noted that simulator sickness is polysymptomatic (Kolasinski, 1996). That is, no single symptom appears in a greater quantity across their test subjects, there is no dominant symptom, and VR sickness symptoms are difficult to measure.

Humans experience the world in very different ways. If cue theory is to be believed, the cues may work under an entirely different set of parameters per person. The way one person moves could vary dramatically from a disabled person, for example, which may mean a difference in the perception of cues. There are so many potential cues, with influence levels varying from person to person, combined with individual physical factors, and a huge number of variables we need to factor in. This is by no means an exhaustive list, but listed are some of the variables in play.

Vection

It is well known that a camera system involving a lot of movement is likely to induce VR sickness. According to research, it may be associated with something known as vection. Vection is the illusion of peripheral movement, and it has been found to be a strong contributor to VR sickness. That is, you feel like you are moving purely through visual cues but you are, in fact, standing still. Spatial discordance is when your visuals disagree with what the inner ear is detecting, and this certainly ties in with the whole cue conflict theory.

Hettinger et al. in 1990 hypothesized that vection must be experienced before simulation sickness occurs (Kolasinski, 1996). They took 15 subjects. Ten were reported as sick. Subjects reported either a great deal of vection or none. Out of the five subjects who did not report vection, only one felt ill. Out of the 10 subjects who reported vection, eight reported feeling sick.

Field of View

A wider field of view produces more vection. Andersen and Braunstein (1985) found that reducing the field of view helped to reduce ill effects, even in cases where the vection illusion was increased. A reduced central visual field meant that only 30% of subjects experienced motion sickness. Note that this is not about changing the field of view setting on a Unity Camera, but instead the amount of visibility around the center of focus.

More recently, in 2016, researchers at Columbia University, Ajoy S. Fernandes and Steven K. Feiner, tested a method of reducing field of view dynamically to reduce sickness (Fernandes and Feiner, 2016). They used Unity to adapt an existing VR demonstration so that whenever the viewer moved around the scene, the field of view would be lessened by an overlay. Visibility is reduced the more the viewer moves around in the virtual world. When the viewer comes to a stop, the field of view opens up again and removes the restriction. By reducing the field of view in this way, their hypothesis was that the restrictor helped subjects have a more comfortable experience and be able to stay in the virtual world longer. Also, as a bonus most subjects also reported that they hardly even noticed the changing field of view restrictor as they moved around.

Interpupillary Distance

There has been a lot of emphasis placed on interpupillary distance (IPD), but there is little scientific evidence to suggest that it is a contributing factor of VR sickness per se. An incorrectly configured IPD on the headset can cause eye strain, which will make for an uncomfortable experience regardless. We looked at measuring IPD correctly back in Chapter 2.

Illness

It goes without saying that certain illnesses may be exacerbated by VR. The inner ear may be affected by many medical conditions including colds, flu, or ear infections. Any sort of issue in the ear can directly affect how the brain interprets balance, and how vection might affect a viewer. Tiredness and other illnesses will also play a role in its effect.

Locomotion/Movement

The way that users move around inside the virtual world can be an issue. Faster movement speeds may produce more of a sense of motion—again likely linked to vection—leading to more feelings of sickness. The way that a person perceives motion is important here, too. Some people are more adept at rotational movement than others, for example. Forced movement is almost always a problem for VR sickness sufferers. People do not tend to enjoy having their view moved around automatically for them, as it tends to move in a way that may not be natural to them which can be uncomfortable. If you are building an experience with movement, try to offer an option to move by teleportation if possible (we looked at implementing teleportation with SteamVR in Chapter 4), as teleportation is a comfortable alternative for those affected by movement-based sickness.

Age

Several articles about VR sickness will quote age as a factor, along with gender, but there is no proof to backup this claim. These claims may stem from studies on motion sickness (not simulator sickness or VR sickness), which have suggested that people between the ages of 2–21 are more likely to experience motion sickness. Rather than blindly quoting motion sickness studies, more research is required in VR specifically. Most currently reported findings on age or gender as factors of sickness in VR should be taken with a pinch of salt.

Frame Rate

Stuttering or lower frame rates have been linked to VR sickness. It is commonly accepted by VR hardware manufacturers that the recommended refresh rate for a VR headset is 90 Hz and that needs to be a stable number. When the frame rate drops or stalls, it can be very obvious to the viewer and cause discomfort. Developing comfortable experiences for VR calls for maintenance of a constant frame rate throughout the entire experience.

In a quest to keep the Playstation VR platform at a high quality, Sony initially refused to certify games if they dropped to a frame rate less than 60 fps. To avoid uncomfortable experiences, senior staff engineer Chris Norton stated, "If you submit a game to us and you drop down to 30 or 35 or 51 we're probably going to reject it" (Hall, 2016).

A VR system needs to render at anything between 60 and 90 fps in two eyes (rendering two different images) as well as maintaining a view on the standard computer monitor, which is quite a big ask for a standard midrange gaming PC. For that reason, we need to make sure that this generation of VR experiences is well optimized to run on a variety of systems at an acceptable and steady frame rate.

Depth Perception

Ironic though it may be, the people with the best vision for VR may be the ones most prone to experience motion sickness. People with good depth perception will experience more of a sense of vection in the virtual world, which may increase susceptibility to sickness (Allen et al., 2016).

Rate of Linear or Rotational Acceleration

Acceleration needs to make sense to the viewer. Smoothing out of acceleration and deceleration can be unnatural when it is applied to human movement. In older First-Person Shooter game titles, camera movement (which was intended to simulate the player's view from their head in the game) tended to be smoothed to a high degree, giving a sort of a sliding feeling for a short period after a movement key has been released. In reality, this type of smoothing is unrealistic and may be uncomfortable when applied to movement in VR.

As with all of these cues, the type of movement affects people in different ways. One of the most basic methods for reducing its effect is to move slower. Not so much that you are edging around the environment, but to try to avoid zooming around at high speed rates. Removing acceleration smoothing will help, too. A more abrupt start and stop may not be the nicest visual effect on a traditional monitor view, but in VR, this is a good compromise when trying to reduce sick users.

Positional Tracking Errors

When the tracking hardware fails or the headset moves out of view of the base stations, it can make for an uncomfortable experience as the view wanders randomly away from where it is supposed to be. At the time of writing, I have yet to see a VR experience that tries to keep tabs of this. It may be worth considering programming a system to look out for unexpected movements or movements that fall outside of a threshold.

SITTING VERSUS STANDING

Some people are naturally steady on their feet, others not so much. This can have an impact on the virtual experience.

CAN WE SOLVE IT?

The answer to this is difficult. Treating VR sickness is like fixing leaks in a pipe that just keeps springing new holes. Fix one, find another. That is not to say that it is impossible. For example, we do not yet know what sort of impact Light Field display-based headsets will have for sufferers. Initial findings seem to suggest that the ability for Light Field VR to have the eye focus more naturally can reduce VR sickness. Unfortunately, the Light Field technology is still in its early stages and this claim is unproven at the time of writing.

In terms of movement and spatial discordance, there may be a solution from stimulating the inner ear. A process called Galvanic Vestibular Stimulation (GVS) zaps the inner ear with tiny electrical impulses to simulate vibrations, which convince the brain that movement is happening. These "patterns" of inner ear vibrations need to be interpreted and recreated, which could mean that the current level of GVS is limited in the types of stimulation it can recreate. Over time, though, we may be able to recreate all of the patterns we need for dynamic experiences. Samsung, creators of the Entrim 4D headphones, hopes that GVS is the answer to solving VR sickness. At the time of writing, Samsung claims to have developed 30 different movement patterns.

A different approach, yet similar idea, is to stimulate the inner ear with constant vibration. This has the result of flooding the inner ear with noise, which may remove the emphasis on processing the inner ear as such an important part of the brain's movement cues. Ototech claims that their device has no adverse effects and that it has the effect of test subjects appearing to be more comfortable with simulated movement.

At the time of writing, there is no medically proven solution, and traditional motion sickness cures have had limited success in VR. Although we do not have the answers, we can at least reduce the impact of VR sickness with technical solutions and workarounds.

It is important for developers to keep VR sickness sufferers in mind when creating their universe. And equally important for them is to stay up-to-date on advancements or new approaches to the subject. We still have a lot to learn. Sharing knowledge is important as we all try to navigate the new medium. The rules of VR are only just being written, and we, the early adopters, are ambassadors of this exciting new technology. The potential for the virtual experience falls far beyond how we see it today. The potential impact of VR for medical, psychological, treatment, and research is incredible. VR can change the world for the better. We need to work together and share findings, to keep VR as an open platform as far away from corporate interest as possible, and collectively make it a better technology for our future.

RECAP

In this chapter, we have focused on VR sickness and looked at some of the most current research findings to help understand what it is we are up against when it comes to VR's worst enemy. I have added my personal experience to this chapter, but it is important to remember that the way one person experiences VR may be completely different from the next. Humans are complex creatures made up of many different components that may be differently sized, have varying sensitivity, or reduced functionality. Variation between just a few of the components we use to judge depth, distance, or balance can mean that one person's comfortable experience may be another person's VR barf-o-rama!

I touched briefly on why there is not yet a medical solution to the problem but how we can try to create more comfortable experiences through sharing our findings and implementing workarounds.

In the next chapter, we will look at some practical methods and Unity implementations to help create VR experiences more comfortable for people susceptible to sickness.

CHAPTER 10

Hands-On, Practical Techniques for Reducing VR Sickness in Unity

USING UNITY'S UI CANVAS FOR FIELD OF VIEW (FOV) REDUCTION

Researchers at the Computer Graphics and User Interfaces Lab of Columbia University found that the effects of virtual reality (VR) sickness were reduced by controlling the range of visibility, based on how much the user is moving around in the virtual world (Evarts, 2016). They used a mask in front of the camera, to provide a view like looking through a hole in a piece of card (Figure 10.1). When the user moved around, the mask was scaled down so that the viewing hole grew smaller. When the user stopped moving, the hole returned to its original scale and, as a result, the FOV was restored. You may have seen a technique like this in the Google Earth VR application (available free on Steam), where the view is masked out whenever you fly around. Another example of this FOV reduction system can be found in the VR game Eagle Flight (published by Ubisoft). In this section, we will look at one way to implement a similar system that will display an image in front of the camera, scaled to dynamically adjust visual range as a target GameObject moves around a Scene.

FIGURE 10.1 The example project for this chapter uses a mask image to reduce the field of view during movement.

Open the Example Project

Open the example project, VR_Chapter_10_Project1—FieldOfView. It contains a Scene named main, which you can find inside the Scenes folder in the Project browser. Open the Scene.

The FOV Mask

The objective of the mask (Figure 10.2) is to provide a visible area in the center and to mask off the rest of the screen. We will scale the image up or down, depending on the movement speed of the object we are tracking, which will reduce or increase the size of the hole in the center and, as a result of that, the visible area for the viewer.

Here's how it works:

1. A Canvas shows the mask image, positioned just in front of the camera so that it is inside the view of the VR camera.

2. The MaskScaler script Component is attached to the image. The MaskScaler will track the movement of the vehicle GameObject in the Scene.

3. The vehicle moves around. The MaskScaler script figures out how fast the vehicle is moving and changes the scale of the mask image if it finds that the vehicle is moving. When the vehicle is moving, the mask gets smaller which, in turn, lowers the visibility in

FIGURE 10.2   The image used for masking the field of view.

the scene—growing the amount of screen covered in black and shrinking the transparent circle in the center.

4. When the vehicle stops moving, the mask scales back toward its original size (which lets the entire view to be visible).

To create the image, I used a program called Paint.Net. It is an amazing free software provided under a Creative Commons license, for editing and creating art. You can download it from http://www.getpaint.net/download. html. If you can afford it, please do donate if you find it useful because the developers rely purely on donation to fund future development.

The mask image for the example project is 1,024 pixels in width and 1,024 pixels high. To make it, I used the Paint Bucket tool to fill the entire image with black. Next, I used the Paintbrush tool with a large-sized brush with a (very) soft edge to create a white circle in the center of the image. To make a brush soft, you just set the Hardness level right down. To get the circle size right, it was trial and error all the way! When it was too small, it did not matter how I scaled it inside Unity—I could see that the area was too small. When it was too large, the effect was almost unnoticeable without scaling down the image so much that its edges became visible.

If you decide to make your own mask image, play around with different sizes to see what works for you.

Finally, I exported the image as a .PNG format image and imported it into the project to use as a UI overlay. In Unity, the shader used to make this image transparent is a Multiply shader normally used for particle effects.

In the example project, click the Canvas GameObject in the Hierarchy and you can see that the Plane Distance is set to 0.31. The trick here is to position the image just far enough from the camera so that it does not get distorted by its projection across both eyes, but close enough to the camera to avoid clipping other 3D objects in front of the camera. This can be tricky depending on the conditions of your own project (how close the viewer's head gets to objects and so forth), so you will most likely need to tweak the distance value if you employ this method elsewhere. If you use any other camera views (such as a spectator camera) you can stop the mask showing up in the other views by placing it on its own layer and choosing not to render that layer to any cameras other than your headset view.

Programming the Dynamic Scaling Script

You can find this script attached to the MaskImage GameObject in the Hierarchy in the main Scene—in the Inspector, it appears as the Component named MaskScaler. The script in full looks like this:

```
using UnityEngine;
using System.Collections;

public class MaskScaler : MonoBehaviour
{
        public Transform objectToTrack;
        [Space(10)]

        public float maskOpenScale = 2.82f;
        public float maskClosedScale = 0.5f;

        public float maxSpeed = 0.04f;
        public float transitionTime = 0.5f;

        [Space(10)]
        private float moveSpeed;
        private Vector3 lastPosition;
        private float theScale;
```

```
        private Transform myTransform;
        private Vector3 myScale;

        void Start()
        {
                // grab some info we are going to need for
each update
                myTransform = transform;
                myScale = transform.localScale;

                // set the default value for the scale
variable
                theScale = maskOpenScale;

                // start out with the mask open
                myTransform.localScale = (Vector3.one *
maskOpenScale);
        }

        void Update()
        {
                // figure out how fast the object we are
tracking is moving..
                moveSpeed = Mathf.Min ( (objectToTrack.
position - lastPosition).magnitude, maxSpeed);
                lastPosition = objectToTrack.position;

                // calculate what percentage between 0 and
max speed we're currently moving at
                float maxUnit = (100.0f / maxSpeed);
                float t = ((moveSpeed * maxUnit) * 0.01f);

                // now use that percentage to figure out
where the target scale should be
                theScale = Mathf.Lerp(maskOpenScale,
maskClosedScale, t);
                Vector3 targetScale = (Vector3.one *
theScale);

                // finally, we lerp the localScale
property of our transform towards the target scale
```

```
        myTransform.localScale = Vector3.
Lerp(myTransform.localScale, targetScale, Time.
deltaTime * transitionTime);
    }
}
```

Script Breakdown

The namespaces we use here are the standard ones Unity includes with all new C# scripts and the class derives from MonoBehaviour so we can tap into the Start() and FixedUpdate() functions Unity will call automatically.

```
using UnityEngine;
using System.Collections;

public class MaskScaler : MonoBehaviour
{
```

The next part of the script contains the variable declarations:

```
public Transform objectToTrack;
    [Space(10)]

    public float maskOpenScale = 2.82f;
    public float maskClosedScale = 0.5f;

    public float maxSpeed = 0.04f;
    public float transitionTime = 0.5f;

    [Space(10)]
    private float moveSpeed;
    private Vector3 lastPosition;
    private float theScale;

    private Transform myTransform;
```

In the variable declarations, you may also notice the [Space(10)] lines—this is a neat little Unity feature that will put a little space between variables when they show up as fields in the Inspector window. Their only purpose is to make the Component look a bit neater when we edit its properties in the Unity editor.

Next up, the Start() function has a little setup in it:

```
void Start()
{
        // grab some info we are going to need for
each update
        myTransform = transform;

        // set the default value for the scale
variable
        theScale = maskOpenScale;

        // start out with the mask open
        myTransform.localScale = (Vector3.one *
maskOpenScale);
    }
```

The Start() function grabs a reference to this object's Transform to avoid having to do any lookup during the main loop. We hold this in myTransform. myTransform will be used by the main part of the script when we need to modify the Transform's scale.

Our mask needs to start out in the open state, so we do not see it, so theScale and the localScale of the mask is set to the open values at the end of the Start() function.

Calculations take place in the Update() function:

```
void Update()
{
        // figure out how fast the object we are
tracking is moving..
        moveSpeed = Mathf.Min ( (objectToTrack.
position - lastPosition).magnitude, maxSpeed );
        lastPosition = objectToTrack.position;
```

Above, the first thing we need to do in Update() is to calculate the current speed of the object we are tracking—the vehicle. We find the speed by taking the current position of the object and subtracting the last position of the object (its position at the last update) to give us a vector. The magnitude (length) of this vector works as our measure of speed that can be used to figure out the mask scale we need.

The last part of the code block above stores the position in lastPosition to use for that distance check the next time FixedUpdate() is called.

The next code block takes the current speed and calculates a scale:

```
        // calculate what percentage between 0 and
max speed we're currently moving at
        float maxUnit = (100.0f / maxSpeed);
        float t = ((moveSpeed * maxUnit) * 0.01f);

        // now use that percentage to figure out
where the target scale should be
        theScale = Mathf.Lerp(maskOpenScale,
maskClosedScale, t);
        Vector3 targetScale = (Vector3.one *
theScale);
```

This system uses percentages to translate the difference between speed and size. In the line:

```
float maxUnit = (100.0f / maxSpeed);
```

maxUnit is a single unit—a single percentage worth, if you like—of speed where 0% is a speed of zero and 100% is maxSpeed. Now that we have a unit to work with, we can take that and multiply it by the current speed, to give us the current speed as a percentage value—we store it here in the variable t:

```
float t = ((moveSpeed * maxUnit) * 0.01f);
```

There's also a multiplier here—0.01f—to bring down the percentage to a value between 0 and 1. The reason for that will become clear in the explanation for the next line:

```
theScale = Mathf.Lerp(maskOpenScale, maskClosedScale,
t);
```

The Mathf.Lerp function is described in the Unity documentation as "returning an interpolated float result between two float values." That is, we give it two values—in this case, a maximum scale (maskOpenScale) and a minimum scale (maskClosedScale)—and then we feed it an interpolation value between 0 and 1. The result back from Mathf.Lerp will be between the two values based on that interpolation value—for example, if the interpolation value was 0, we would get back the value of maskOpen-Scale. If the interpolation value was 1, we would get the value of mask-ClosedScale. If we were to pass in 0.5, we would get whatever value is midway between the two and so on.

The Mathf.Lerp function takes in a value between 0 and 1, so to be able to use our speed percentage value as the interpolation value, then the percentage needed to be scaled by 0.01. Our percentage is now a value between 0 and 1, ready to use with Mathf.Lerp.

With the scale worked out, we then convert it over to a Vector3:

```
Vector3 targetScale = (Vector3.one * theScale);
```

Finally, with the scale set as a Vector, we can easily use targetScale to set the .localScale of our Transform (via the reference in myTransform):

```
            // finally, we lerp the localScale
property of our transform towards the target scale
            myTransform.localScale = Vector3.
Lerp(myTransform.localScale, targetScale, Time.
deltaTime * transitionTime);
```

Rather than setting the scale directly, which would cause the scale to grow and shrink instantly depending on speed, we Lerp (interpolate) between the Transform's current scale and our new target scale. Using Time.deltaTime (the time between updates) multiplied by an arbitrary value in transitionTime, we had an interpolation value based on time that should transition the mask scale at the same speed regardless of frame rate/machine speed.

That is the end of the MaskScaler.cs script. In the Scene, you will find it attached to the MaskRawImage GameObject, which is a child object of the Canvas GameObject.

Try Out the Example

Press Play to preview the Scene.

Remember that you may need to recenter the camera if the headset view starts out in the wrong place. We looked at the VR_Config.cs script (which takes care of recentering and making sure that SteamVR is set up for a seated experience) back in Chapter 8 of this book. The VR_Config script is attached to the [CameraRig] GameObject.

When you drive the vehicle around the Scene, the visibility will change depending on your movement. When you stop moving, the view should open. Start moving, it should close to restrict the view.

The researchers at Columbia University were able to find the right speed of transition where several of their test subjects did not even notice when the FOV closed. I played around with the settings here quite a lot but did not reach the same level of quality reported by the researchers. My time was limited, but perhaps you can manage to find a nicer balance (feel free to let me know if you do—I am on Twitter and I would love to hear about it).

In Eagle Flight (Ubisoft), they use an FOV mask with settings much stronger than this example. If you see the mask in a video, in stills, or anywhere outside of VR, it may appear to be extremely obvious, but it is not always the case. When you are involved with the action, immersed in the experience, you would be surprised by how strong you can make the mask before it becomes obtrusive. For the masking system to work, it needs to mask. So, do not be afraid to push it a little further by reducing its transparency to a more obvious level.

An Alternative Approach

Before we close this section and move on to third-person cameras, although I will not be covering it here I wanted to mention that you may also want to consider using a fixed-size image and setting its alpha values somewhere between 0 and 1 rather than its scale. This method works just as well as scaling a mask, and it has been used as one of the comfort options available in the VR game title FREEDIVER: Triton Down by Archiact.

To achieve this, you could use the same code we used for this to calculate the speed percentage. Then, use the 0.01f multiplier to turn the percentage into a number between 0 and 1 and use that to set the alpha value of the color on the mask material.

Another thing you may want to consider—if your simulation uses a lot of rotation—is to add the rotation speed to the mask scale calculation. The specifics for how you go about this will vary depending on how your vehicle or character rotates, but to summarize one way would be to get the magnitude of rotation and add that to the moveSpeed value before it is converted into a percentage. In some cases, you may be able to just do that for a single axis of rotation rather than having to work out the magnitude. It depends on the simulation.

A THIRD-PERSON CAMERA SUITABLE FOR VR

As we have seen in games like Lucky's Tale, by Playful, Inc., it is possible to make a fun and comfortable third-person experience in VR that can be enjoyed by just about everyone; including people who might normally get sick from VR. In their VR Developers Conference talk, in March 2016, Dan Hurd and Evan Reidland from Playful, Inc., outlined their approach to designing the levels and camera systems for Lucky's Tale (Hurd and Reidland, 2016).

One of their key observations was the importance of getting the camera movement just right. VR sickness symptoms may be triggered by the character stopping in place but the camera continuing to move. They found that, if the camera does not appear to exist in the same context as the player, moving in the same way, it appears to cause disconnect between the two, leading to an uncomfortable feeling for the viewer. The key here is to make sure that the camera stops and starts as we expect it to, and not to follow the player around uniformly. When the player stops moving, we want the camera to stop moving too. This is counter to what you would normally see in game camera behavior. The Lucky's Tale VR game used a velocity-based follow camera. Normally, the camera would move independently of the target's speed, following the target around the environment at its own speed of movement. Instead, here we use the camera target's speed and apply that same speed to the camera.

The way the camera moves around and follows its targets has a significant impact on the comfort of the experience. What Playful did with Lucky's Tale VR was to fix the camera rotationally, so that it always points in the same direction. The lack of turning the camera helped to reduce VR sickness. Levels were designed around the camera's fixed orientation to stop clipping through scenery or the player from being fully obscured by set pieces.

In this section, we build a camera based on the one from Lucky's Tale. It will not only use the velocity of the target (the player) but also has an optional amount of interpolation so that can lag behind the target a little, if required. The interpolation will reduce any jerkiness if your player starts or stops suddenly. The rotation of the camera will not be set at all, left up to the viewer's headset rotation instead.

Open and Try Out the Example File

Start by opening the example project for this chapter, which you can find in the folder named VR_Chapter_10_Project2—3rdPerson. Making an entire game is beyond the scope of this book, but the example here is a third-person arena game. Emphasis will be on the camera system only. Graphics are taken from Unity's old demonstration project—AngryBots— and most of the game code can be found in my book C# Game Programming Cookbook for Unity 3D (Murray, 2014).

So, what is it? The game works like this; Several robots spawn into the arena, and the main character can move around and fire a blaster to blow up the robots. That's all there is to it!

In the SCENES folder, there are two Scenes named game_LBS and start_LBS. To try out the game, open the start_LBS Scene and hit Play with your headset on. Remember that you can reset the camera to its correct position at any time, by pressing the R button. Use a game controller or arrow keys on the keyboard and Z to fire the blaster.

Programming

In the Project browser, open the scene named game_LBS in the SCENES folder. This is the main game scene, where we can look at how the camera is being moved around and so forth. The script in this section is applied to an empty GameObject acting as a parent object to the camera itself. This allows us to easily offset the position of the camera from the target. The target is our character avatar running around the virtual world.

In the Hierarchy, find the GameObject named CameraParent.

Click on CameraParent so that you can see it in the Inspector. Right click on the VR_Cam Component in the Inspector and choose Edit Script from the dropdown menu.

Here is the script in full:

```
using UnityEngine;
using System.Collections;

public class VRCam : MonoBehaviour {

    private Vector3 directionVec;
    private Vector3 targetPosition;
    private Vector3 currentPosition;
    private Vector3 targetVelocity;
    private Vector3 currentVelocity;

    public float targetSpeed = 2;
    public float maximumVelocity = 3;
    public float acceleration = 1;
```

```
    public Transform followTarget;

    private Transform myTransform;
    private Rigidbody myRB;

    void Start()
    {
        myTransform = GetComponent<Transform>();
        myRB = GetComponent<Rigidbody>();
    }

      void Update ()
    {
        currentPosition = myTransform.position;
        targetPosition = followTarget.position;

        // grab direction vector
        directionVec = targetPosition
- currentPosition;
        targetVelocity = directionVec * targetSpeed;

        // clamp velocity
        targetVelocity = Vector3.ClampMagnitude
(targetVelocity, maximumVelocity);
            currentVelocity = Vector3.MoveTowards
(currentVelocity, targetVelocity, acceleration * Time.
deltaTime);

        myRB.velocity = currentVelocity;
    }

    public void SetTarget(Transform aTransform)
    {
        followTarget = aTransform;
    }
}
```

Script Breakdown
The script starts with:

```
using UnityEngine;
using System.Collections;

public class VRCam : MonoBehaviour {
```

The class derives from MonoBehaviour, as we will update movement within the Unity-called Update() function. As you can see in the code above, we do not need to use any packages other than the standard packages added automatically by Unity (UnityEngine and System. Collections).

The variable declarations are next:

```
private Vector3 directionVec;
private Vector3 targetPosition;
private Vector3 currentPosition;
private Vector3 targetVelocity;
private Vector3 currentVelocity;

public float targetSpeed = 2;
public float maximumVelocity = 3;
public float acceleration = 1;

public Transform followTarget;

private Transform myTransform;
private Rigidbody myRB;
```

I will explain the variables as we continue through the script. Next, the Start() function takes care of a little setup:

```
void Start()
{
    myTransform = GetComponent<Transform>();
    myRB = GetComponent<Rigidbody>();
}
```

Nothing unusual in the code above. We just grab references to the GameObject's Transform and Rigidbody Components so that they can be used further down in the script. You will see myTransform and myRB appearing in the Update() function below. The Update() function is the core of our class, where all of the position calculation takes place:

```
void Update ()
{
    currentPosition = myTransform.position;
    targetPosition = followTarget.position;
```

To find the current velocity of the player, we need to know where both of our main objects are, in the 3D space. currentPosition holds the position of the camera and targetPosition holds the place of the target object that we want the camera to follow around.

```
// grab direction vector
directionVec = targetPosition - currentPosition;
targetVelocity = directionVec * targetSpeed;
```

DirectionVec is a Vector3, found by getting the difference in position between where we are and where we want to be. In the code above, we get to the direction vector by subtracting the current position of the camera from the position of the target.

To find out how quickly we want to move the camera around, a value to store in the targetVelocity variable, the next line takes directionVec and multiplies it by the targetSpeed variable. targetSpeed is a float used by the developer (us) in the Inspector, to tweak the camera speed. directionVec contains the direction we want to move in, and targetSpeed contains the speed we want to get there at.

```
// clamp velocity
targetVelocity = Vector3.ClampMagnitude
(targetVelocity, maximumVelocity);
```

The movement needs to be clamped to a maximum, so that it does not go too fast. As developers, we need control over the maximum speed to be able to make sure that the experience stays comfortable. Zipping the camera around the scene at high speed would be a sure-fire way to require barf bags.

To clamp the motion, here we use Vector3.ClampMagnitude, which takes a vector to represent the original vector you want to clamp, and a float to represent the maximum length of vector for the ClampMagnitude function to return. The magnitude (the length from point to point) of the vector returned by Vector3.ClampMagnitude will be at the value in maximumVelocity. maximumVelocity is public so that the developers can alter this value in the Inspector easily.

```
currentVelocity = Vector3.MoveTowards
(currentVelocity, targetVelocity, acceleration * Time.
deltaTime);
```

currentVelocity is calculated inside the Vector3.MoveTowards() function. The Unity documentation describes MoveToward as moving a point in a straight line toward a target point. We take the currentVelocity and move toward the targetVelocity at a maximum distance of acceleration * Time.deltaTime. The variable acceleration is a float type variable, set by us earlier in the variable declarations or via the Inspector, to control the movement effect.

Unity gives access to its timing system via the Time class and Time. deltaTime is the time between this frame and the last frame. By multiplying our acceleration value by the Time.deltaTime, it provides a time-friendly value that will retain steady movement regardless of computer speed or any potential glitches in frame rate. This value is used to tell Vector3.MoveTowards how far to move each time this code runs. The vector returned by MoveTowards is held by currentVelocity, which is used in the next line to set the velocity of our rigidBody:

```
        myRB.velocity = currentVelocity;
    }
```

The last part of the script is the SetTarget() function:

```
    public void SetTarget(Transform aTransform)
    {
        followTarget = aTransform;
    }
```

The SetTarget() function is there specifically to fit in with the game-specific code. The game code spawns the player into the scene and then needs a method to tell the camera about the player object, so that the camera can follow it around the scene as the game is played. The GameController script finds the main camera GameObject and uses GameObject. SendMessage (a Unity-provided function) to call the SetTarget() function, passing in the Transform of the player as a parameter. The variable followTarget is set to the transform passed in by the game code and the camera can then follow it around.

The Third-Person VR Camera Rig

With a script in place on the CameraParent GameObject, we should take a little look at the Inspector to revise the structure and see how it looks in the editor (Figure 10.3).

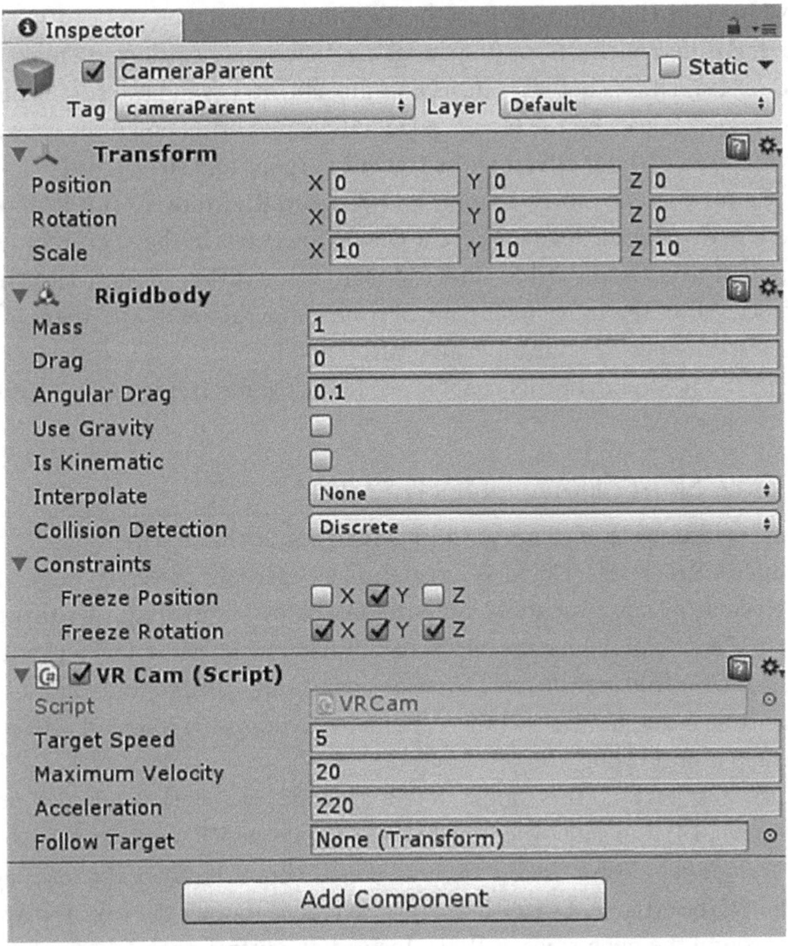

FIGURE 10.3   The third-person camera component in the Inspector.

The VR Cam Component has three parameters. Those are

Target Speed: This is the speed we are consistently trying to get to.

Maximum Velocity: This is a limit on how fast the camera can move around.

Acceleration: The camera can gather up speed slowly or quickly toward its target speed. If the acceleration value is too low, you may find that the camera sometimes overshoots its target and takes too long to accelerate back in the opposite direction to follow its target.

By changing the parameters on the VR Cam Component, you can achieve several different effects to suit your game. Lower acceleration will make for slower transitions between stasis and movement. If you have slower moving targets, lowering the target speed will help to bring down the speed of the camera without affecting the transition speed and so on.

CameraParent moves around and [CameraRig] moves with it. If you were to expand the CameraParent GameObject out in the Hierarchy, you would find the standard SteamVR prefab [CameraRig] in there as a child object. All of the movement control is on CameraParent, and there is no movement-specific code on [CameraRig] at all.

In the next part of this chapter, we look at something a little unusual: a fake nose.

A FAKE NOSE? HOW DOES IT SMELL?

One of the more bizarre sounding theories is that a virtual nose can reduce VR sickness. David Whittinghill, an assistant professor in Purdue University's Department of Computer Graphics Technology, says that the virtual nose can reduce the effects of simulator sickness by 13.5% (Venere, 2015). Dr Whittinghill says, "You are constantly seeing your own nose. You tune it out, but it's still there, perhaps giving you a frame of reference to help ground you."

In this part of this book, I will provide you with a virtual nose (Figure 10.4) and show you how to apply it to your VR simulations.

It does not always need to be a nose, as we know it. The VR game Eagle Flight (Ubisoft) uses a shape like a nose to reduce motion sickness as players fly around the open skies of Paris. Instead of a literal nose, the developers chose to position a beak (you are, after all, playing as an eagle) where the

FIGURE 10.4　The virtual nose sits in the center of the view, barely visible.

player's nose might normally be. The beak substitute nose is believed to help players in the same way as a regular nose shape might. If you are unsure about using a big schnozzle, perhaps try another similar shape to see if you can achieve a similar effect.

Sufferers of VR sickness also seem to get along better with a cockpit around them, and it may be down to the same principal of a virtual nose, having a static reference point.

Open the Example Project

Open the example project for this chapter, folder Chapter 10—Project 3—Nose.

Grab your headset and hit Play to test out the Scene. You will notice that it is not quite possible to focus on it. That is the intended effect. It is supposed to work in a similar way to the visibility of a regular, real nose, in that we are constantly aware of its presence but unable to look at it in detail. Inside the VR headset, you should be able to see the nose if you close one eye and look at it, but it should not be too visible when you look straight ahead.

To change the nose color, find the Materials folder in the Project browser. Click the NoseSkin material. In the Inspector, to the right of the word Albedo is a little color swatch (a square of color). Click on the color swatch to show the color picker and choose your new nose color. As this Material is already applied to the nose in the prefab, the nose in your Scene should update automatically as you select colors.

Some may find this whole nose business distracting, whereas others may find it helps, so perhaps the best way to implement a virtual nose is to allow viewers to switch it on or off. In this case, you can toggle nose visibility by pressing N. The script NoseToggle.cs takes care of toggling the GameObject of the nose mesh on or off and you can find it attached as a Component to the Nose GameObject, which is in the Hierarchy location: [CameraRig] > Camera > Nose.

The nose provided with this book is what I like to think of as a starter nose. It may be enough to demonstrate the concept, but you could probably source a much nicer nose elsewhere. Again, we only need it to be there not to be the perfect in-focus representation of a real nose. The virtual nose is there to help try to trick the brain into having one of its regular reference points back. You could also try out a few different nose shapes and sizes, too, so that people can choose how prominent the nose will be in their view.

RECAP

In this chapter, we looked at building a third-person camera that should make for more of a comfortable experience for viewers. Following on from that, we looked at another technique for reducing the effects of vection by reducing the FOV with an overlay. The final part of this chapter looked at adding a virtual nose. It may seem a little outlandish, but research suggests that it can make a difference in some subjects. This brings us back to a point made in the previous chapter, in that we may not be able to stamp out VR sickness for everyone, but we can at least provide some tools to lessen its effects. Something as silly sounding as a virtual nose may be just the right cue for someone out there to feel more comfortable, so it is worth consideration if your simulation is going to be out in public where you do not know who will be experiencing it. The shape of the nose, its color, and visibility may have different effects for different people. Try to sniff out the best solution and do not blow it when you pick the nose.

In the next chapter, we take a brief look ahead to the future and wonder where things might be going from here.

CHAPTER 11

Unity Engine Polish and Optimization

OPTIMIZING UNITY FOR VR

A difficult part of virtual reality (VR) development is cramming everything into the simulation without destroying performance. VR calls for your graphics hardware to do more than it was originally intended for—certainly, more than rendering a single image to a 2D screen. For VR, two images need to be rendered—one for each eye. The images are updated faster than a lot of common monitors will even display at. At its current level, the quality of experience we strive to achieve is pushing the limits of the hardware we have, and it is important to optimize our work as much as possible. Keeping the frame rate high, responding quickly to input and providing smooth, intuitive interfaces are the key to providing a comfortable nausea-free VR experience for your users. It can sometimes be difficult to achieve, but Unity provides some tools to help make it happen, and with a little caution it is possible to deliver high-end experiences.

THE RENDERING STATISTICS WINDOWS (STATS)

Your journey to optimization starts with the Stats window (Figure 11.1), which is accessible by the Stats toggle button in the top right of the Game view.

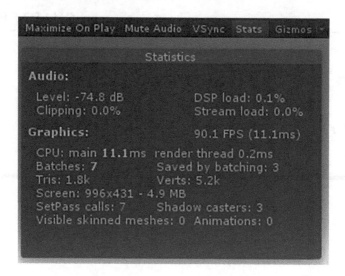

FIGURE 11.1 The Stats window shows running statistics in the Game view.

The information shown in the stats window contains

CPU—Main: This is the time that it takes to process and render a single frame of the Game view. This timer does not include time taken by the editor to do its thing—only how much time it took to put together a frame of the Game view.

Render Thread: This is the time taken to render a single frame of the Game view, without processing. This is only how long it takes to render.

Batches: This tells us how many objects have been batched together in terms of sending their data to be rendered.

Saved by Batching: This number is how many render passes have been saved through the process of batching. It is a good indicator of how much the batching optimization process is helping in your Scene.

Tris and Verts: Triangles and vertices make up the entire 3D world. Although rendering technology is extremely good at dealing with them, you should always be wary of pushing the tris and verts counts too high.

Screen: This is the current resolution of the Game view, along with the antialiasing level and memory usage.

SetPass: The number of rendering passes. A high SetPass number will impact performance negatively.

Variable Skinned Meshes: This is the number of skinned meshes being rendered in the Game view.

Animations: The number of animations running in the Scene.

CPU vs. GPU

Although the graphics hardware needs to work hard to be able to render VR at a good, steady frame rate, you also need to keep an eye on how hard the computer's processor is working. The CPU (Central Processing Unit) takes care of most of the code-based processing like game logic, whereas the GPU (Graphics Processing Unit) works with rendering or, in some cases, physics simulation. If the CPU is working too hard, we call it CPU bound. If the GPU works too hard, it is GPU bound. By using the profiler (Figure 11.2), you can find out which one it is.

The Unity Profiler

As the application runs, the profiler collects information about all the elements—scripts, shaders, audio, and so on—to display information about how they are using resources. With a little knowledge, the Profiler can help you to find out where performance can be improved.

You can open the Profiler window through the menu Window > Analysis > Profiler (or the keyboard shortcut is CTRL+7). With the Profiler window open, Unity will record performance data and display it on the graph.

Profiler Modes

Along the top of the Profiler (ignoring Add Profiler button for now, but we will get to that further down) are some of the modes the profiler can operate in (Figure 11.3):

Record: Start or stop performance data recording. Performance will be profiled whenever this button is checked and the Profile window is active (either open or hidden behind another tab, but not closed).

Deep Profile: The profile will record many different aspects of the simulation, but if you wanted to get in-depth and have the editor record levels from all scripts and objects you will need to enable Deep Profiling. Deep Profiling monitors everything going on in the application, and you can enable it by clicking on the Deep Profile button from the bar of buttons at the top of the Profiler window. The downside to deep

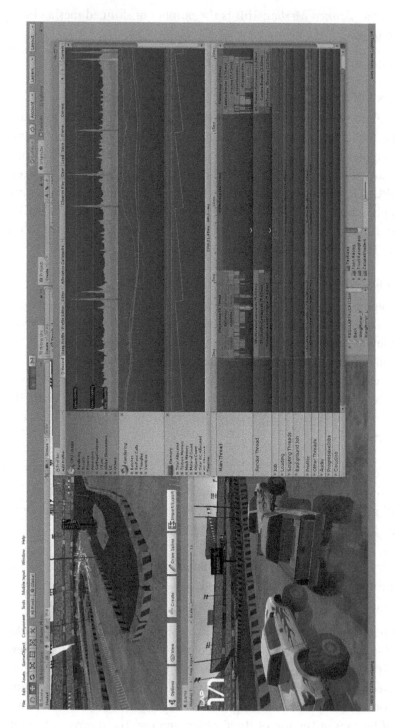

FIGURE 11.2   The Profiler.

FIGURE 11.3 The buttons across the top of the Profiler allow you to customize and choose the level of profiling.

profiling is that you will be unable to do much when it is profiling because of the amount of resources and memory the process takes. Your project will likely drop down to just a few frames per second as Unity times every single line of code being executed, and every element being rendered or manipulated by the engine.

Profile Editor: This toggles whether or not to include the Unity editor in the performance data recording. Under normal circumstances, you can leave this unchecked but if you decide to use or build editor plugins or extensions, it can come in super-handy to make sure everything is behaving as expected.

Editor: This is used for remote profiling, where you can choose the IP address of a Player to profile.

Allocation Callstacks: Clears the Profiler window of all recorded performance data.

Clear: Clears the Profiler window of all recorded performance data.

Clear On Play: Whenever this is checked, Unity will clear the Profiler window of all recorded performance data whenever you press the editor's Play button.

Load: Loads profiling data from a (previously saved) binary file. It can also be appended to any existing data by holding down Shift on the keyboard when you click this Load button.

Save: Saves profiling data to a binary file. This can be useful to use for comparison after you have made changes to your work to make it perform differently. For example, you might load back saved data to see which areas have been improved upon performancewise.

Different Profilers   In the Profiler window, down the left-hand side of the graphs are the active profilers. In the top left of the Profiler window is a button Add Profiler. You can choose what gets profiled and focus on areas that might need attention or choose to profile a multitude of different aspects. Unity does offer a wide range of profilers:

CPU

GPU

Rendering

Memory

Audio

Video

Physics

Physics2D

Network Messages

Network Operations

UI

UI Details

Global Illumination

Finding Out If Your Project Is GPU-Bound or CPU-Bound

When the CPU finishes all the tasks it needs to perform in an update, it must wait for the GPU to complete all its tasks too before moving on to the next update. This waiting period is normally unnoticeable to us humans, but if we look at it under the Profiler it can help us to see whenever the GPU is taking too long and holding up the CPU. By looking at this delay in the Profiler, we have a method to know which side of the system is having to work the hardest and where to start in squeezing out some extra performance from our projects.

Open a project you would like to profile.

Open the Profiler window through the menu Window > Analysis > Profiler (or keyboard shortcut is CTRL + 7).

With the Profiler open, press the Play button in the editor to start playback and profiling. As soon as playback begins, you should start to see data being captured by the Profiler.

Count to around 20 seconds to capture some data, then pause playback in Unity.

The Profiler takes the form of a timeline. When there are spikes in the graphs or high points, we can pause Unity and move/scrub the playhead (a white line on the timeline) to examine specific moments where performance seems to be hit the most. For now, though, we just need to find out about that waiting period on the CPU.

The bottom of the Profiler window shows an Overview timeline of what the CPU profiler is registering (Figure 11.4). This gives us a great visual overview, but we need to look at specific scripts and objects by switching this view over to Hierarchy.

Click on the dropdown just above the Overview (by default, this will read Timeline, but it could be Timeline, Hierarchy, or Raw Hierarchy). From the dropdown, choose Hierarchy.

With Hierarchy selected, the view should change to show a hierarchical view of everything the CPU profiler has been monitoring (Figure 11.4). By expanding out the various categories, you should be able to find individual scripts in your project and see how they are performing. The Total percentage values tell you how much of a tick that task is occupying. The higher the percentage, the more processing that script is taking up in relation to other scripts. That said, it is perfectly acceptable to have a single task taking up a large percentage of time if everything is performing well. These numbers are here to show you what is taking up the CPU cycles, and it is up to you to decide where you can improve or whether they need to be improved. Besides the Total column, there is also a Time column.

Hierarchy				CPU:21.46ms GPU:--ms			No Details
Overview	Total	Self	Calls	GC Alloc	Time ms	Self ms	
EditorLoop	53.7%	53.7%	2	0 B	11.55	11.55	
PlayerLoop	44.9%	0.2%	2	219.2 KB	9.64	0.06	
Camera.Render	17.5%	0.3%	1	0 B	3.76	0.07	
Update.ScriptRunBehaviourU	5.3%	0.0%	1	226 B	1.14	0.00	
PreLateUpdate.ParticleSystem	4.0%	0.0%	1	0 B	0.87	0.00	
FixedUpdate.ScriptRunBehav	4.0%	0.0%	1	0 B	0.86	0.00	
PreLateUpdate.ScriptRunBeh	3.0%	0.0%	1	218.9 KB	0.65	0.00	
FixedUpdate.PhysicsFixedUpc	2.8%	0.0%	1	0 B	0.60	0.01	
PostLateUpdate.UpdateAllRer	1.4%	0.0%	1	0 B	0.31	0.00	
EarlyUpdate.PhysicsResetInti	1.3%	0.0%	1	0 B	0.29	0.00	
PostLateUpdate.UpdateAllSki	0.8%	0.0%	1	0 B	0.18	0.00	
PostLateUpdate.ParticleSyste	0.7%	0.0%	1	0 B	0.16	0.00	
PostLateUpdate.UpdateAudio	0.5%	0.0%	1	0 B	0.12	0.00	
FixedUpdate.AudioFixedUpda	0.5%	0.0%	1	0 B	0.12	0.00	
PreLateUpdate.DirectorUpdat	0.5%	0.0%	1	0 B	0.11	0.00	
PreLateUpdate.DirectorUpdat	0.3%	0.0%	1	0 B	0.06	0.00	
GUI.Repaint	0.1%	0.0%	1	0 B	0.03	0.01	
PreUpdate.PhysicsUpdate	0.1%	0.0%	1	0 B	0.03	0.00	
EarlyUpdate.UpdateInputMan	0.1%	0.1%	1	0 B	0.02	0.02	
UGUI.Rendering.RenderOver	0.0%	0.0%	1	0 B	0.01	0.00	
FixedUpdate.NewInputFixedU	0.0%	0.0%	1	0 B	0.01	0.01	
EarlyUpdate.UpdateMainGam	0.0%	0.0%	1	0 B	0.01	0.00	
Initialization.PlayerUpdateTin	0.0%	0.0%	1	0 B	0.01	0.00	

FIGURE 11.4 The CPU Profiler can breakdown the performance of individual tasks and scripts.

Click on the title at the top of the Time column to sort by time (how long each task took to execute). We want this to be in descending order, so make sure that the arrow next to Time ms is pointing down. If it points up, click Time again.

Find the task Gfx.WaitForPresent. You may have to scroll down to find it. If you find that Gfx.WaitForPresent is taking up a lot of time and sitting near the top of your Overview, it may be that the GPU is taking too long and your project is GPU bound.

If Gfx.WaitForPresent is not taking up too much time and you are still seeing performance issues, it would suggest that your project is CPU bound.

What Do the Squiggles Tell You?

The Profiler window takes the form of a timeline, showing performance data recorded by any active profilers. You can click on the timeline and drag around to see the data recorded at specific times.

The list down the left side of the window is the available profilers, with the currently selected category highlighted—the currently selected category will take over the timeline. Profilers in the profiler list are active and recording whenever the profiler is recording, but the data shown in the graph belong to the currently selected profiler only.

Profiler Types   The different available profilers:

CPU: The CPU is the main processor. This is the place to track scripts and see how they are performing.

GPU: The GPU refers to the processor on the main board of the graphics card. This Profiler allows you to see how the GPU load is being distributed. In the Profiler graphs, different types of rendering are color coded, such as rendering transparent textures or shadows.

Rendering: The Rendering Profiler sheds light on how much time is spent doing the actual rendering and how the time is being spent on getting the data to the graphics card. The graph is color coded to show batches, SetPass calls, triangles, and vertices separately.

Memory: It is important to look at memory in conjunction with the other Profilers. Low memory can affect performance; when the memory is full, the computer is forced to move things around to accommodate new assets and so forth: wasting precious CPU cycles. Check the amount of RAM (Random Access Memory) on your system or your target system specification and compare it to the results you see here.

Memory usage should go up and down during runtime, as objects and assets are loaded into memory and unloaded as required. If any of the numbers keep increasing as your project runs, this is known as a memory leak. In the case of a leak, you will need to find the object(s) and stop them from being created. Memory leaks will, eventually, cause your project to run slowly, and over time, it will cause a crash.

When you select the Memory Profiler, useful information is shown at the bottom of the window in the Overview area:

Used Total	The amount of memory your Unity project takes up, in total.
Unity	The amount of memory that the Unity editor is taking up
Mono	How much memory the Mono libraries take.
GfxDriver	My graphics driver uses around 4.3 MB. Find out what yours uses here!
Audio	Audio can be a memory drain. Keep an eye how many audio files you use, the compression rate they use, and how long they are.
Video	Video files can eat up memory quickly if the compression rate is very high. Try to avoid playing video files at the same time as doing anything too performance hungry.
Profiler	Profilers will take up a chunk of memory with all the data needed to store and process.
Reserved	An amount of memory will be reserved by Unity to avoid other programs from taking over too much of the RAM. Unity looks at the numbers of objects and assets in the project, and their sizes, to calculate a memory estimate. The estimated amount is then used to reserve enough memory to be able to load everything in comfortably.
Textures	In VR, there is a tendency to use the highest texture sizes possible to be able to examine objects at close range without the textures looking blurry and compressed. Keep an eye on these numbers!
Meshes	Mesh information (the model with no texture data) is rarely a problem in terms of memory, but if you have important architectural models or extremely detailed 3D models, you should be aware of memory usage.
Materials	Materials are the information that links shaders, textures, and meshes. Although materials do not use up much RAM, if you have an excessive amount of them and this value is particularly high you will need to reduce them.
AnimationClips	Generally animation clips do not use up a lot of memory, but Unity does give the option to compress animations if you find that they are using up a lot of memory. Reducing the number of key frames in an animation can also help reduce the file sizes.

(*Continued*)

AudioClips	Be aware of how much memory your audio is using if you are using a lot of high-quality audio clips. Audio can use a lot of memory, especially long music or ambient clips.
Assets	This number is a count of the total assets used by your project and loaded in memory at the current point in the timeline.
GameObjects	In Scene, although GameObjects do not use a huge amount of RAM, if this number is too high, you may also run into performance issues from additional processing. The higher this number is, the more chance of performance is being impacted though perhaps not always due to memory alone.
Total Objects in Scene	This includes types of objects other than GameObjects, such as scripts instances. As with GameObjects, there will be an overhead for the number of Objects in a Scene, even though they usually do not take up a large amount of memory.
Total Object Count	The total number of Objects created. If this number rises as playback continues, it may mean that your project is creating Objects that are never destroyed (also known as a memory leak).

Audio: The performance impact of a few sounds may be small, but once your audioscape gets more complicated it can really begin to affect things. The Audio Profiler lets you know about the sounds in play and how they affect memory, CPU usage, and so on. For performance reasons, also keep a check on how many audio clips you are playing at the same time and be wary of loading large clips (such as long music or ambient audio) into memory at the same time.

Physics: Overloading the physics engine will slow things down. The Physics Profiler lets you know some useful statistics about what the physics engine is up to and how all the physics objects are behaving. The Profiler counts the following properties:

Active Dynamic	The number of nonkinematic Rigidbodies. Nonmoving Rigidbodies can also go into a "sleep" mode to preserve processing. This number will not include any sleeping Rigidbodies, as the physics engine does not process on them.
Active Kinematic	This is the number of nonsleeping kinematic Rigidbodies. Physics joints can also increase this number, as Rigidbodies may need to be processed multiple times for joint physics (always be wary of this if you are using a lot of joints).
Static Colliders	The number of Colliders on GameObjects that are not Rigidbodies. As an example, static colliders in a racing game might be the walls around the track but not the vehicles.
Rigidbody	The total number of Rigidbodies, regardless of state.

(Continued)

Trigger Overlaps	Triggers have collision processing like regular colliders, except for the fact that, with a trigger, there is no physics correction/impact. Too many triggers will impact performance.
Active Constraints	The number of primitive constraints processed by the physics engine.
Contacts	Unity documentation states that this is "The total number of contact pairs between all Colliders in the Scene, including the amount of trigger overlap pairs as well." Essentially, then, Contacts is how many objects are touching.

Physics 2D: Unity is also used for 2D games. The 3D and 2D physics are dealt with by two different physics engines inside the one engine, so profiling the 2D physics needs to be done separately by the Physics 2D Profiler.

Network Messages: When you are making multiplayer or networked projects, the Network Message Profiler will help to determine where and how network resources are being spent.

Network Operations: When you are making multiplayer or networked projects, the Network Operations Profiler provides profiling of network-specific functions like synchronized variables and Remote Procedure Calls (RPCs).

You can drag and drop the Profilers to reorganize them, remove them (e.g., to focus on specific areas without the performance overhead of unwanted profilers), or add new profilers from the Add Profiler button.

Using the Profiler

Bear in mind that the Profiler is a tool. It does not tell you where the problems are, it is just a method for seeing how your project is performing. You need to do a little detective work.

If your project is performing badly, you can use the Profiler to find the heaviest performance loads and look to improve them using some of the methods in the next part of this chapter.

Batching

When the renderer puts images together to display on the screen, it must process each piece of geometry, lighting information, all the shaders and textures, and send the data to the display system. The GPU works on the graphics card to deal with graphics processing and the CPU deals with everything else. The two combined are extremely powerful and capable of some amazing things, but VR is extremely demanding for both. A huge challenge for the hardware is in moving the massive amounts of data—all those meshes, shaders, and textures take up a lot of bandwidth. In the game engine, we have a measure known as rendering passes. For the record, Unity developers used to refer to draw calls for performance, which have been replaced by rendering passes. Put simply, a rendering pass count is how many times we have to send information about objects to be drawn to the GPU. Keeping down the rendering pass count is vital to reducing bandwidth and keeping performance at a good level. Unity provides a batching system built-in, which can combine multiple draw calls into a single call whenever they share common features such as using the same material. When meshes remain in a single place, they can also be grouped together as static geometry and sent in a single pass.

Occlusion

Sometimes, not all a 3D environment's nonmoving objects will be visible to the viewer. There may be obstacles between objects and the camera, or the camera may be looking in another direction. So why render them all, even when they may not be visible?

Occlusion culling is the process of skipping the rendering of static objects whenever they are not visible to the camera, whether that means out of the camera's visibility range or hidden behind other object(s). Unity's occlusion culling system has been refined down to a straightforward setup process that will help you to squeeze out some extra frames per second with just a small amount of work.

Try Occlusion Out with the Example Unity Project

Open the example file for this chapter in Unity: Chapter13_Project_ Occlusion. Find the Scenes folder and open up the Scene named occlusiontest.

The main camera sits inside an approximate circle of 3D cubes (Figure 11.5). We will set up the occlusion culling system to hide any cubes out of the view of the camera.

First, we need to tell the engine which objects are static. Occlusion culling only works with static objects.

Click on one of the cubes in the Scene view, so that it shows up in the Inspector. In the top right of the Inspector is a checkbox labeled Static (Figure 11.6). Check the box.

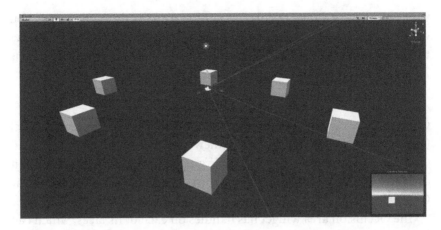

FIGURE 11.5 In the example project for this section, the main camera is surrounded by cubes.

FIGURE 11.6 For GameObjects to be culled, they must be marked as Static in the Inspector.

Repeat the procedure for the remaining cubes. They all need their Static checkboxes setting to true for this to work. Note that if, for whatever reason, you only want to set the object to static for occlusion purposes only, use the Static dropdown menu to select individual static properties.

The Occlusion Panel Open the Occlusion panel via the menu Window > Rendering > Occlusion Culling. The Occlusion panel will open as an extra tab over the Inspector.

At the top of the window is a small section for Scene filtering. The available options are All, Renderers or Occlusion Areas, and the default setting is All. In that Scene Filtering section, click Occlusion Areas and you should notice that the Hierarchy empties, as Unity filters out any type of object that is not an occlusion area. As there are no occlusion areas set up now, the Hierarchy is empty.

Occlusion areas are used to tell Unity which areas to use in culling. This means you can pick and choose which areas should be affected by it. There is nothing to stop you from just hitting the Bake button in the Occlusion panel and letting Unity calculate occlusion data for the entire scene. You do not strictly need any areas if you intend for occlusion culling to affect the entire Scene. We will cover adding an occlusion area here, anyway, as it may not always be the case that you will want to cull an entire Scene.

Adding Occlusion Areas

Click the Create New (Occlusion Area) button in the Occlusion panel (Figure 11.7). In the Scene view, a new green cube should appear; an Occlusion area widget—this is a visible guide to the Occlusion area, and it can be dragged and dropped around, resized and such, just like a regular GameObject.

The Occlusion area widget has handles on each of its faces, which can be used to resize it. You can use the regular object move mode to drag them around. Grab the handles on the side faces and pull them out, so that the area covers all the cubes around the camera (Figure 11.8). Be sure to make the occlusion area large enough to cover the cubes horizontally and vertically. You can go a little larger than you need to, for this exercise.

The occlusion area will be used to calculate visibility data, which is then used at runtime to decide which models are visible and which ones are not and, in turn, which objects to render, and which ones not to. If your camera finds its way outside of the occlusion area, the occlusion culling will not work, and everything will be rendered at once. You need to make sure that anywhere the camera might go is covered by the occlusion area.

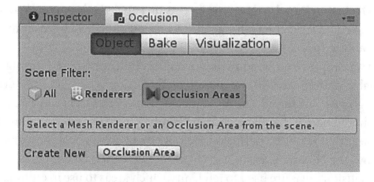

FIGURE 11.7 The Occlusion panel appears as a panel in the same part of the editor as the Inspector.

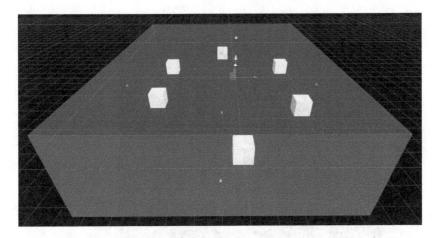

FIGURE 11.8 The occlusion area widget needs to cover all the objects to be included for occlusion.

Bake the Occlusion Cells

Back in the bottom right of the Occlusion panel is a Bake button. Click Bake to have Unity go ahead and calculate the occlusion data. The Scene window will change. These are the data cells that Unity's occlusion culling system uses to create something known as binary trees. Binary trees can be a complex subject beyond the scope of this sentence, so we will leave it at that here. You can easily find some good information about binary trees online, if you are interested in digging deeper.

Try It Out

We want to be able to see the culling as it happens in the Scene view, but still be able to see what the camera sees in the Game view. Before you press Play, check that the Maximize On Play checkbox, located above the Game view, is not checked. The editor layout should show both the Game view and Scene view at the same time. Make sure that the small Occlusion Culling panel, at the bottom right of the Scene view, has its dropdown set to Visualize (Figure 11.9).

Press Play to preview the Scene. The camera will rotate based on the mouse position. Move the mouse left or right and notice how the cubes in the Scene view appear and disappear, depending on their visibility.

Occlusion culling is least useful for game environments that are combined into single large meshes and most useful when you are making an environment with separate objects that may be easily hidden or rendered.

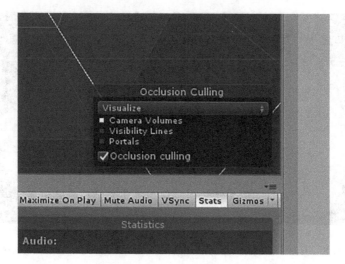

FIGURE 11.9 When the small Occlusion Culling panel is set to Visualize, any culling carried out by the currently active camera will be shown in the Scene view.

Unity's terrain system will also be affected by occlusion culling, which helps a lot when trying to generate frame-rate-friendly scenes featuring terrains.

Quick Code Tips

Cache Object References

The most important code tip I can pass on is to cache all of your object references that are accessed with GetComponent() in regularly called code or functions like Update(), FixedUpdate(), or LateUpdate(). If you are referencing transform or GameObject repeatedly, you may end up negatively impacting performance. It is a lot more efficient to declare variables to store references in.

Here, we will compare two versions of the same mouse rotation script from the "Occlusion" section of this chapter. The script is added to the camera as a Component and acts to rotate the camera around about its y axis based on the mouse position.

The bad way:

```
using UnityEngine;
using System.Collections;

public class MouseMove : MonoBehaviour {

    private Vector3 tempVec;
```

```
    void Update () {
        // get the current eulerAngles from this
GameObject
        tempVec = GetComponent<Transform>().
eulerAngles;
        // set the y to the mouse position
        tempVec.y = Input.mousePosition.x;
        // now, set our GameObject's eulerAngles
to the one with added mouse pos
        GetComponent<Transform>().eulerAngles =
tempVec;
    }
}
```

The right way:

```
using UnityEngine;
using System.Collections;

public class MouseMove : MonoBehaviour {

    private Transform myTransform;
    private Vector3 tempVec;

    void Start () {
        // cache the ref to the Transform for
speed
        myTransform = GetComponent<Transform>();
    }

    void Update () {
        // get the current eulerAngles from this
GameObject
        tempVec = myTransform.eulerAngles;
        // set the y to the mouse position
        tempVec.y = Input.mousePosition.x;
        // now, set our GameObject's eulerAngles
to the one with added mouse pos
        myTransform.eulerAngles = tempVec;
    }
}
```

In the two scripts above, the first thing you may notice is that there is a bit more work involved in caching the reference. That may be off-putting and when you are working to get things done quickly, the bad way may look like a more attractive proposition. Sure, it may be easier, but the performance hit could show up in Profiling, and it is always better to err on the side of caution and do it the right way!

In the bad way, we use the command transform to find the Transform Component attached to the same GameObject as this script. There have been limited independent tests by Unity users to see if using the .transform of a GameObject is any faster and, at the time of writing, although using .transform is faster than calling GetComponent() every frame, it is still slower than caching the reference. This may change in the future, but again—erring on the side of caution is probably the best way to approach this and any performance increase, no matter how small it will be, is beneficial to your project in the long term.

Prioritize Where in the Update Cycles Your Code Runs

When using MonoBehaviour-derived classes, there are some functions automatically called by the game engine at different times in its update cycles. For performance, you should put a little thought into where you code runs—as an example, you might not need minor UI updates to run in a function that gets called multiple times per frame. It would be more efficient to run this code in LateUpdate, after everything else is done.

There are several functions (Unity calls these Messages) which, as a part of Monobehaviour, will be called automatically by the game engine:

Awake(): When the script instance is being loaded, Awake() is called. This makes it the best place for initialization that does not rely on other GameObjects (since other GameObjects may not have been initialized at this stage). It is also the best place to put any GetComponent or GameObject.Find calls to cache references.

Start(): This is called before any updates are called, at the start of the Scene after the script instance has loaded. It will only be called once by Unity.

Update(): The Update() function is called every frame. You cannot rely on the timing of it, so you either need to implement your own timing or avoid updating positions or physics here.

FixedUpdate(): Called every fixed framerate frame. The fixed time step can be set via the menu at Edit > Settings > Time > Fixed Timestep.

The frequency of calls to FixedUpdate can be higher than the number of calls to the Update function, depending on fixed timestep vs. fps settings. As FixedUpdate's frequency can be more than Update, it is often called multiple times per frame, and a bad choice for any code could potentially impact performance. The FixedUpdate function should be reserved for physics updates or anything that specifically needs to be called in FixedUpdate due to timing reasons. Try to keep everything out of FixedUpdate!

LateUpdate(): Called after all Update functions have been called, including FixedUpdate, this is useful for dealing with objects or events occurring after main or physics updates. For example, camera code is likely best placed in LateUpdate because cameras usually look to objects that have moved during the main loop.

OnEnable(): This function is called whenever the object becomes enabled and active.

OnDisable(): This function is called whenever the object is disabled.

Only Run Scripts When You Need To

Another useful optimization tip is to disable GameObjects when you do not need them to do anything. For example, a script that moves a GameObject to a target position no longer needs to run the movement script once it reaches its destination. The script can be disabled once it reaches there, by using

```
this.enabled = false;
```

Another similar method is to use a Boolean variable to wrap up code in your main function that will only be set to true whenever you need the main code to run. For example, imagine a robot non-player character (NPC) moving around the environment. In the main loop, we have a Bool variable named isFarAway. When isFarAway is false, we run the main movement code. When it is false, we skip all main updates and the robot will stay in its place. The player can move far away from the robot, so we do a quick distance check to see how far away the robot is from the player and, depending on the result of that, isFarAway is set to true or false. This helps in two ways; far away robots do not waste CPU time on their movement or pathfinding, and we will not have to update all of the robots in the Scene at the same time—only the ones close enough to matter.

Geometry and Modeling

As mentioned earlier in this book, VR is extremely demanding in terms of hardware requirements and how hard your PC will be pushed by rendering the virtual world. As we are at such an early stage of VR, the types of experiences we are aiming to achieve are right at the top end of what most computer hardware can deal with. Most VR-spec graphics cards will be pushed to render what we accept as normal on desktop systems, in a virtual world alternative. Anything we can do to reduce the load, within a reasonable compromise of quality if we must, is going to be a big help.

Materials

Texture atlasing is the process of using a texture map that contains several different textures combined into a single image (Figure 11.10). The large multitexture is mapped to more than one surface or 3D object differently,

FIGURE 11.10 A texture atlas combines multiple textures into one, saving memory and helping to increase performance. (Courtesy of Kenney Game Assets—https://www.kenney.nl.)

reducing the number of times that the CPU is required to send texture data to the GPU and reducing draw calls. Reducing draw calls will, in turn, improve performance.

Sadly, texture atlasing is not just a case of combining textures. It calls for the way that the 3D models are UV mapped to be tiled to suit. A 3D artist should plan to UV map in this combined way before starting the texturing phases, as it is harder to retexture a model for an atlas after it has been textured for individual image mapping.

Although this is a complicated technique, the returns can be huge performancewise, as atlasing reducing SetPass calls. The less SetPass calls, the better the rendering performance.

Level of Detail (LOD)

As a 3D model moves further away from the camera, its details are less visible. There is little point in rendering a highly detailed model when it is so far away that all its details will be lost, so Level of Detail (LOD) provides a solution. Many videogames use a process known as LOD to draw different versions of models based on their distance from the main camera. Usually, each model is the same shape but containing different detail levels, where as you get closer the more detailed meshes are used and as you move further away the less detailed meshes are used. This takes a degree of strain off the processing—possibly reducing the number of meshes, reducing the number of triangles that need to be drawn, the draw calls, and possibly the total texture sizes required to render the current camera view.

LOD calls for the 3D artist to produce multiple versions of the same mesh, but the performance boost in complex games is huge. Most commercial games employ some kind of LOD system—if you have ever played any 3D games from the early 2000s you may have seen something called "popping in," where the switches between levels of details are very obvious and create a sort of popping effect as the environment around the main camera constantly changes. Nowadays, we usually employ a fading effect to use transparencies and fade between meshes of different levels of detail—often with smart use of fading, the correct distances, and clever positioning, it is possible to almost completely hide the switching process from the viewer.

Unity has a built-in option for LOD grouping. To take advantage of it, you first need to create a set of meshes with names ending in _LOD followed by a number—for example, CAR_LOD0, CAR_LOD1, CAR_LOD2, CAR_LOD3, and so on—for as many LOD levels you want to provide. Unity assumes that 0 is the most detailed model, with LOD numbers increasing with lower detail models in the higher numbers.

When you import a sequence of meshes like this, an LOD group for the object with appropriate settings will be created for you automatically. When you add the main model to the Scene, it should already have an LOD Group Component attached to it (Figure 11.11), but if you need to, you can add an LOD Group Component via the Add Component button in the Inspector. You can find it under Rendering > LOD Group.

LOD Groups are used to manage level of detail (LOD) for GameObjects. With the LOD Group Component, you can change where the LOD models get switched out and add a fade effect between the transitions.

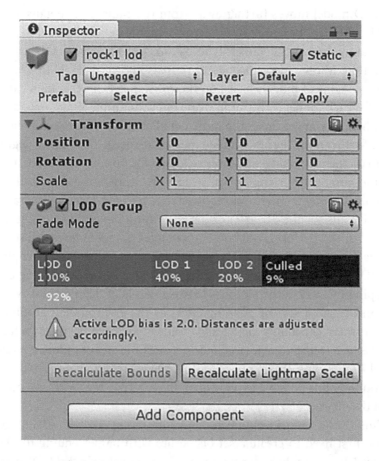

FIGURE 11.11   The LOD Group Component configures how the LOD system will choose which mesh to render.

There are also two global LOD settings that can be found in the Quality Settings menu inside the Unity editor Edit > Project Settings > Quality. In quality settings, there are two settings applicable to LOD. These are LOD Bias and Maximum LOD Level:

> *LOD Bias:* The LOD Bias setting determines how an LOD system will decide which level to use when it needs to decide between two levels. A lower bias leans toward less detail, and a higher number more than 1 leans toward using the higher quality levels.
>
> The Unity documentation provides the example where setting LOD Bias to 2 and having it change at 50% distance (set on the LOD Group Component), LOD only changes at 25%.
>
> Maximum LOD Level Models below the maximum LOD level are not included in the build, which means we can customize the LOD system for the type of device you are building for without having to rebuild or change your higher-end device-ready LOD setup. Lower-end devices might not require the highest detail levels, and the maximum LOD level means you can drop it down so that only the lower quality levels will be used in the build.
>
> *Automated LOD:* If building the separate meshes seems like too much work, you may want to look at purchasing one of the automated solutions. One such solution might be Simple LOD by Orbcreation, which is available from the Unity Asset Store and can generate LOD meshes and carry out automatic setup with very little work. There are a few other LOD solutions and tools available on the Unity Asset Store, such as Automatic LOD by Ultimate Game Tools—it really depends on budget, what you are looking for, and what exactly you are hoping to achieve.

Lighting

Lighting is an expensive process, but it can be optimized.

Lightmapping

Lightmapping is the process of precalculating all the lighting information for static parts of a 3D environment, so that the data can be reloaded at runtime and light the scene with very little overhead. A 2D image file known as a lightmap contains a black and white image that is applied to models in the Scene just as though it were another material, except the lightmap serves only to texture 3D models with light rather than patterns or images. With lightmapping applied to your Scene, you no longer need to light it dynamically, therefore, saving a lot of processing at runtime.

You will need to have Baked Global Illumination checked in the Mixed Lighting section of the Lighting Settings (Window > Rendering > Lighting Settings). You can also change lightmapping settings in the Lighting Settings window.

Through baked lighting, you should be able to lower the amount of required active lights at runtime which will in turn improve performance.

Per-Pixel vs. Vertex Lighting

Per-pixel lighting is a lovely technique that calculates lighting for every pixel on the screen. It looks great, but it can be a performance drain especially when you use many of them. Unity also supports something called vertex lighting, which is a less realistic way of lighting objects but calls for a lot less processor power to pull off. You can tell Unity how many per-pixel lights are allowed by setting the Pixel Light Count value under Rendering in the Quality section of Project Settings—Edit > Project Settings.

Quality Settings

It is a good idea to offer quality settings so that a wider range of systems will be capable of running your experience smoothly. You can tweak quality settings in the Quality section of Project Settings—Edit > Project Settings so that each quality delivers the best visual settings based on how your project is structured.

You should offer settings of at least low- and high-quality values. To change the quality through code, you can use the QualitySettings class. Each quality setting is represented as an index number, which will depend on how many quality settings you have set up in the Quality section of Project Settings:

```
QualitySettings.SetQualityLevel (index,
applyExpensiveChanges);
```

applyExpensiveChanges should be true or false. These are things that will potentially cause a stall when the settings are changed, such as turning on or off antialiasing.

As an example, the default set of quality settings offers six different levels. Zero would be the lowest quality, with five as the maximum "ultra" quality level. If we wanted to set the quality to ultra and allow expensive changes, the statement to do it would be like this:

```
QualitySettings.SetQualityLevel (6, true);
```

The QualitySettings class offers several other functions such as being able to get all of the available quality levels to iterate through in code. It also provides access to individual rendering quality settings like turning on or off VSync and so forth. If you want to add an advanced quality menu allowing users to turn rendering features on or off themselves, the QualitySettings class is the way to go for that.

Collisions, Mesh Colliders, and the Layer Collision Matrix

Despite how good Mesh Colliders are for accurate collisions, using a lot of them can cause performance degradation. Before adding a Mesh Collider to a GameObject, first make sure that it absolutely needs a Mesh Collider and that you could not achieve the same effect with a primitive Collider like the Sphere or Box Colliders. If your mesh calls for a Mesh Collider, use convex and adjust the SkinWidth in the Inspector to get a lower poly collision mesh.

Only allow collisions between necessary objects by using layers for all your physics GameObjects and the Physics Layer Collision Matrix (Edit > Project Settings > Physics) to decide which layers can collide with each other. Doing this will reduce the amount of processing required for collisions as the game engine runs. The Layer Collision Matrix can get quite complicated in bigger projects (Figure 11.12), so it is important to name your Layers descriptively.

For example, in the game Axe Throw VR, unlockable items are delivered in crates that drop down from the top of the environment. To unlock the item, the player must throw an axe at the crate to break it open. For the crate to drop down like a typical physics object, it must be a Rigidbody. The crate only needs to collide with the ground and the axes, so I make a new Layer for the crate (named "Crate") and set the crate GameObject to use the Crate Layer. Once that is done, I set up the Layer Collision Matrix so that crates collide only with the ground and axe layers. If the crate collides with anything else in the Scene, it will be ignored, and no processing will have to be done to resolve the collision.

The Layer Collision Matrix looks a little intimidating, as it is a giant triangle of checkboxes after all, but do not be afraid! Across the top of the

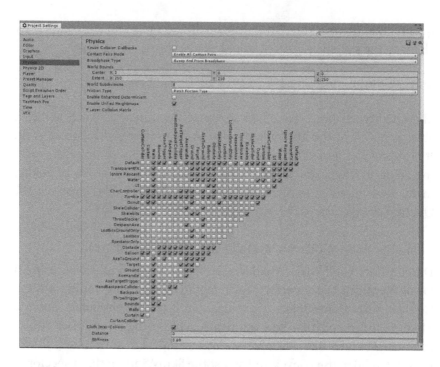

FIGURE 11.12   The Layer Collision Matrix for Axe Throw VR.

matrix are names of all the Layers in your project. Down the left-hand side are, again, all the names of Layers in your project. The checkboxes at the intersection of two Layers determine whether they can collide. For example, if you wanted objects on the Zombie layer to collide with objects on the Ground layer, you could first find the Zombie layer down the left side of the matrix and then find the Ground layer name across the top. Imagine a line drawn down from the Ground layer name and another line draw across from the Zombie layer name on the left. Where the two lines cross is the checkbox that decides the GameObjects on those two layers collide.

RECAP

To keep our virtual visitors comfortable and our experiences high quality, visiting Unity's profiler is a good way to find out how to make things run smoother. We looked at the profiling performance with the Profiler in this chapter and looked at something called occlusion. Occlusion means that the game engine only must draw what is visible, saving precious processing time by leaving out any 3D geometry that need not be drawn.

After looking at the occlusion system, we also covered some coding tips and finished off with a few hints and tips on keeping the geometry efficient.

All game projects go through some sort of optimization and polish phase and your VR projects should too. If your VR experience is going out to the public, or it runs on unknown systems, you can never be quite sure how near or far that system will be from the minimum specs recommended by the headset manufacturers. Other factors than the hardware itself often come into play, such as other programs that may be running in the background or any CPU-intensive background tasks that might be running as a part of the operating system. It is our job, therefore, as VR developers, to try to optimize our experiences as much as possible without compromising too much visual fidelity. The frame rates should be as high and as smooth as possible and it may take some work to get there, but it will be work that your audiences will appreciate in the long run. At the very least, you should investigate profiling to make sure that there is nothing silly happening to cause your simulations to run at a speed less than optimal. If you can, try to always schedule polish and optimization time at the end of your project. Make sure that you are not still adding features at this stage, however. The project should be 100% feature complete for final optimization, but there is nothing stops you from scheduling in multiple optimization sessions across its development. Running the profiler, checking the occlusion, and double-checking code for more efficient approaches are something that should ideally be scheduled several times throughout the entire production. Let us be realistic—doing this weekly may be unacceptable in some production environments, but you should at least factor some optimization time into the development schedule, for example as production milestones, if that is how you are working. In VR, keeping the frame rate up is vital. With the current generation of technology, optimization is key to achieving that.

FINAL WORD

Since the first page, this has been a crazy awesome journey. If you have been playing along with the projects in this book, you will have gone right from setting up the hardware and downloading software all the way through to spraying bugs. I like to think that this book has what you need to get up and running with development using SteamVR, whether that is taking just a few pieces or taking it all. One of the reasons I chose to use SteamVR libraries over other specific hardware-provided systems is the flexibility it offers and quality of the software, giving you the widest possible audience and widest number of devices at the lowest cost. Using the SteamVR system means that we only need to manage a single codebase for multiple devices and device types. SteamVR makes for a feature-rich, wide-reaching ecosystem already geared up for solid, social experiences.

Now that we have reached the end of this book, I hope that you can venture out there to bring your VR ideas to life on your next adventure. The virtual space is a place without rules, which makes it the perfect place to get a little crazy and try something different. The rules and conventions we have established in videogames and simulations are there to be built upon or completely rewritten for VR. Do not think for a second that the conventional approach is the best or only way to do something. In the virtual world, it is all unknown. If something feels natural, regardless of what it is or how silly it seems: you should pursue it and see where it goes. A simple crazy idea you have today could become a conventional approach in the future.

Feel free to let me know what you create, because I would love to hear about it. Find me on Twitter @psychicparrot to say hi! Create, explore, have fun, and please always take good care of yourself and everyone else.

Have fun making games!

Jeff.

References

3Dfx Interactive 3D Chipset Announcement. Google Groups. Last modified November 26, 1995, accessed April 11, 2017. https://groups.google.com/forum/?hl=en#!msg/comp.sys.ibm.pc.hardware.video/CIwBRIX9Spw/YQIsql5GwAYJ.

Allen, B., T. Hanley, B. Rokers, and C. Shawn Green. 2016. Visual 3D motion acuity predicts discomfort in 3D stereoscopic environments. *Entertainment Computing* 13: 1–9.

Andersen, G. J. and M. L. Braunstein. 1985. Induced self-motion in central vision. *Journal of Experimental Psychology: Human Perception and Performance* 11(2): 122–132.

Artaud, A. 1958. *The Theatre and Its Double: Essays*. Translated by Mary Caroline Richards. New York: Gross Press.

Doulin, A. 2016. Virtual reality development tips. Gamasutra: The Art & Business of Making Games. Last modified June 14, 2016, accessed April 11, 2017. http://www.gamasutra.com/blogs/AlistairDoulin/20160614/274884Virtual_Reality_Development_Tips.php.

Evarts, H. 2016. Fighting Virtual Reality Sickness. The Fu Foundation School of Engineering & Applied Science, Columbia University. Last modified June 14, 2016, accessed April 11, 2017. http://engineering.columbia.edu/fighting-virtual-reality-sickness.

Fernandes, A. S. and S. K. Feiner. 2016. Combating VR sickness through subtle dynamic. *2016 IEEE Symposium on 3D User Interfaces (3DUI)*. Greenville, SC, 201–210.

Greenwald, W. 2018. The secret to VR development? Cardboard box forts. PCMag.com. Ziff Davis, LLC. https://www.pcmag.com/news/the-secret-to-vr-development-cardboard-box-forts.

Hall, C. March 17, 2016. Sony to devs: If you drop below 60 fps in VR we will not certify your game. *Polygon*. Accessed December 12, 2016. http://www.polygon.com/2016/3/17/11256142/sony-framerate-60fps-vr-certification.

Hurd, D. and E. Reidland. 2016. 'Lucky's Tale': The unexpected delight of third-person virtual reality, a technical postmortem. Video, accessed April 11, 2017. http://www.gdcvault.com/play/1023666/-Lucky-s-Tale-The.

Kisner, J. July 22, 2015. Rain is sizzling bacon, cars are lions roaring: The art of sound in movies. *The Guardian*. Accessed December 12, 2016. https://www.theguardian.com/film/2015/jul/22/rain-is-sizzling-bacon-cars-lions-roaring-art-of-sound-in-movies?utm_source=nextdraft&utm_medium=email.

Kolansinski, E. M. 1995. Simulator sickness in virtual reality. Technical Report. Alexandria, VA: United States Army Research Institute for the Behavioral and Social Sciences.

Kolasinski, E. M. 1996. Prediction of simulator sickness in a virtual environment. Dissertation. Orlando, FL: University of Central Florida.

Kramida, G. 2016. Resolving the vergence-accommodation conflict in head-mounted displays. *IEEE Transactions on Visualization and Computer Graphics* 22(7): 1912–1931. doi:10.1109/tvcg.2015.2473855.

Lang, B. 2016. Touch and vive roomscale dimensions visualized. *Road to VR*. December 5, accessed December 12, 2016. http://www.roadtovr.com/oculus-touch-and-htc-vive-roomscale-dimensions-compared-versus-vs-visualized/.

Lanman, D. and D. Luebke. 2013. Near-eye light field displays. *ACM Transactions on Graphics (TOG)* 32(6). doi:10.1145/2508363.2508366.

Murray, J. W. 2014. *C# Game Programming Cookbook for Unity 3D*. Boca Raton, FL: CRC Press.

Sell, M. A., W. Sell, and C. Van Pelt. 2000. *View-Master Memories*. Cincinnati, OH: M.A. & W. Sell.

Statista. 2016. Virtual reality (VR)—Statistics & facts. *Statista*, accessed December 12, 2016. https://www.statista.com/topics/2532/virtual-reality-vr/.

Venere, E. 2015. 'Virtual nose' may reduce simulator sickness in video games. Purdue University. Last modified March 24, 2015, accessed April 11, 2017. http://www.purdue.edu/newsroom/releases/2015/Q1/virtual-nose-may-reduce-simulator-sickness-in-videogames.html.

Weinbaum, S. G. 1949. *A Martian Odyssey: And Others*. Reading, PA: Fantasy Press.

Wikipedia. "Binary Tree," Wikipedia. *The Free Encyclopedia*. Last modified April 15, 2017. https://en.wikipedia.org/w/index.php?title=Binary_tree&oldid=773837683.

Index

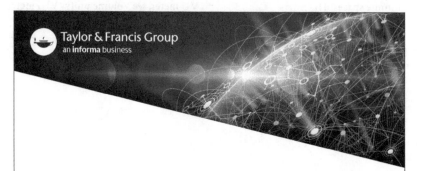